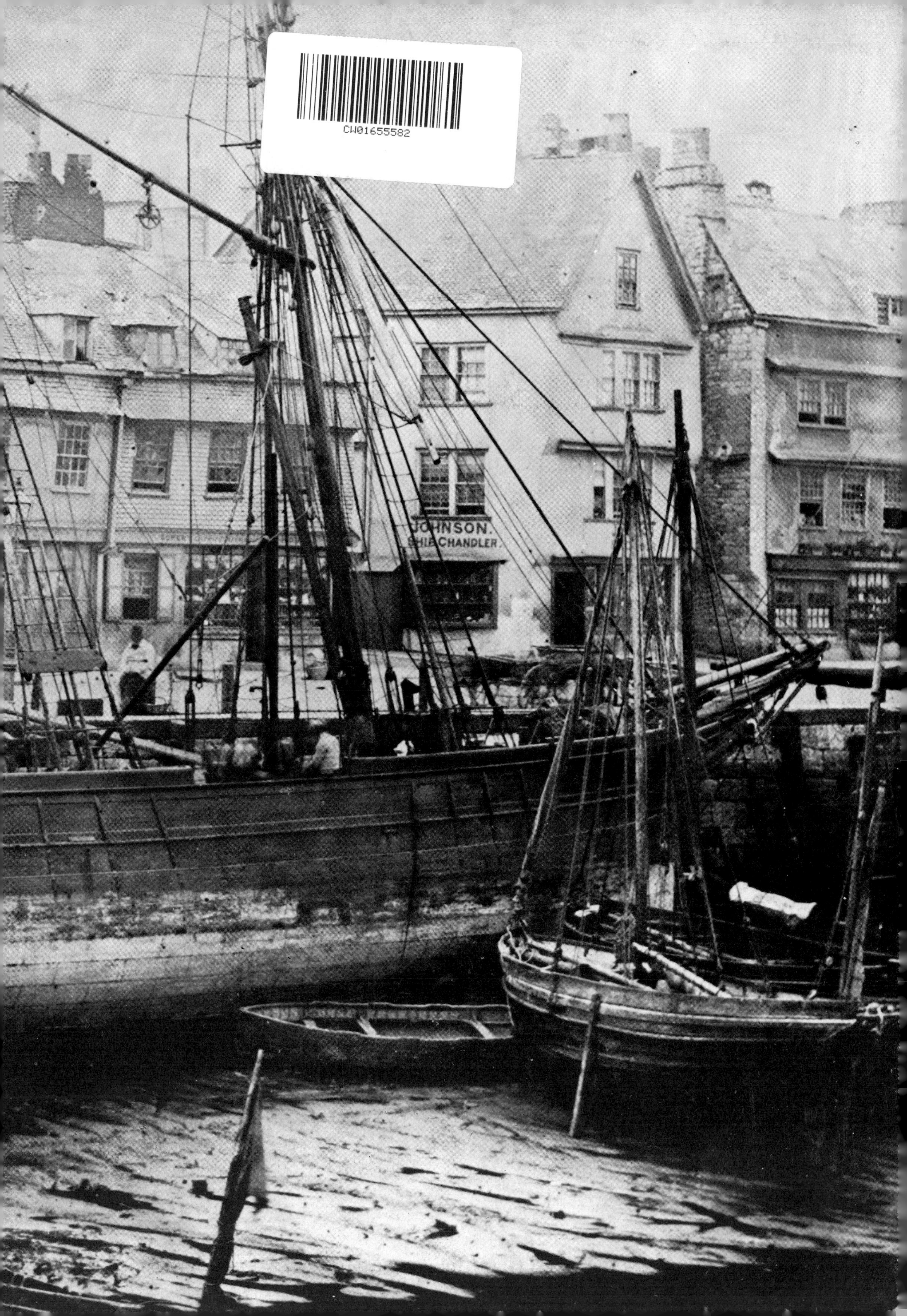
JOHNSON.
SHIP CHANDLER.

Front cover board
Hansom cabs in George Street, c 1868. Louis Duprez
Endpapers. The Barbican Quay c 1865
Men cleaning shot at The Gunwharf, c 1855, *facsimile from an original calotype negative.*

Andrew Cluer
February 1974

ISBN 0 9502853 0 7

First published 1974

Printed in Plymouth
by Hitchings & Mason Ltd.
Cover design by Ron Beer
Western Art Services Ltd.
Preparation and assistance by Alf Menhennett

Original photographs copied by
Central Photos of Plymouth
and Bernard Colgan

Plymouth & Plymothians

PHOTOGRAPHS & MEMORIES

Frederick Gladstone Coles of Plymouth, a keen amateur photographer, captured the attractions of a stall beside the tram line at the turn of the century. Toffee apples and nougat were well worth queuing for. A satisfied customer crosses Hoe Road to the boatmen's shelter where others watch the antics of a puppet show.

LANTERN BOOKS
9 RUTGER PLACE PLYMOUTH

Compiled by
Andrew Cluer

FOR MY WIFE BRENDA

Looe Street, c 1896. R. Monk

ACKNOWLEDGEMENTS

The collections of Plymouth City Library and Museum form the nucleus of this book by courtesy of the City Librarian W. Best Harris Esq. FLA, his colleagues O. A. Baker ALA, K. V. Burns and Mrs. B. R. Cluer BA, the City Curator A. A. Cumming Esq. FMA and J. Barber MA.

Thanks are due for the illustrations from a presentation album in The Mayor's Parlour to The Lord Mayor of Plymouth; for information from Frith's original catalogue and permission to reproduce his photographs to *The Louis Rothman Collection of Victorian Photographs by Francis Frith*; and for the use of photographs in their possession—to The Society for the protection of ancient buildings, Bath Municipal Libraries, Reece Winstone, The Bishop of Plymouth, Sutton Harbour Improvement Company, Lawrence House Museum Launceston, The Western Morning News, The Star Group of Companies, The Port Admiral, H.M. Naval Base Devonport, The Royal William Victualling Yard Museum Stonehouse and The Captain, Royal Naval Engineering College Manadon.

The Author is particularly grateful for the loan of photographs from treasured family albums and vivid memories of life in Plymouth before the blitz, as seen by the man behind the camera to:- J. S. Abrahams, R. Blackett, S. Brimacombe, R. Burt, R. F. Coles, B. Colgan, C. Downey, A. J. Glinn, K. Goodridge, S. H. Hambling, Mrs. Joyce Hellens, J. Hitchings, T. Lacey, Mrs. F. Lawson, Mrs. Mabel Martin, Mashford Brothers, F. Mundell, Miss Elizabeth Norris, R. Phillips, Miss Lillian Phillips, P. W. E. Prance, K. Rickard, R. Serpell, C. Staal, C. Stoneman, B. Swift, F. Tucker, D. Vosper, M. Ware, W. Woodbury, and G. Wycisk.

Ron Jess of Hitchings & Mason Ltd. gave helpful advice during the preparation of the book.

KEYHAM LAKE ROAD
Devonport Gas Works
NAVAL COLLEGE
Keyham Dock Yard
North Basin
Quadrangle Armour Plating &c.
Boscawen St.
Kent Street
Herbert St.
MORICE TOWN
St. James Church
Crosshill Slate Quarry
Saltash Road
Keyham Lane
Underhill
Devonport Leat
Block House
Devonport Water Works
Reservoir
Haddington St.
Keppel St.
Victoria
Bowling Green
Pentillie Villas
STOKE
NAVY ROW
CORNWALL RAILWAY
ALBERT VILLAS
Osborne Road
Osborne Villas
Wingfield Villas
STABLES
Valletort Road
Moons Cove
Cement Works
Tamar Canal
Tamar Quay
Tamar Cottage
Pottery Quay
Ferry Canal
Ferry Road
Torpoint Ferry
Gloucester Street
Milne Pl.
Higher Portland Pl.
Lower Portland Place
Beyrout Pl.
Nelson Villas
Nelson Terr.
MANOR LODGE
Stopford Place
DEVONPORT PARK
Waterloo Place
Wellington St.
Albemarle Villas
Paradise Place
STOKE CHURCH
School
Stoke Church
Fellows Pl.
Tunnel
Carriage Dock
The Camber
Gun Wharf
Devonport Stonehouse & Cornwall Hospital
Granby
Barracks
Devon Militia Artillery Depot
MORICE SQUARE
Ordnance St.
Military Prison
Granby Barracks
Barrier Gate
Drawbridge
Lower Stoke
DEVONPORT
LONDON
Genl. Military Hospl.
DEVONPORT
FORTIFICATIONS
Military Road
Raglan Barracks
Government Ground
CORNWALL ST.
Cannon Street
FORE STREET
Landing Place
North Corner
Reservoir
Chapel
Duke Street
St. John Street
KER STREET
Cumberland Road
Royal Engineers Offices
Devonport Hill
Stonehouse Lake
Tannery
Stonehouse Bridge
Edgcumbe St.
Devonport
Dock Yard
Mast Pond
Building Slips
PEMBROKE STREET
CLOWANCE ST.
Prospect Row
Admiralty Ho.
Magazine
Parade
Government Ho.
Barracks
Telegraph
Battery
MOUNT WISE
Richmond Walk
Royal Clarence Baths
Mutton Cove
Stonehouse Pool
Whitehall
Timber Yard
George Street
EMMA PLACE
Royal Marine Barracks
DURNFORD STREET
Caroline Pl.
HAMOAZE
ROYAL WILLIAM VICTUALLING YARD
Royal Landing Pl.
Victualling Yard Reservoir
Devils Point
Western King
Western King Point
Firestone Ba
Cremill
Edgcumbe Arms Inn
Old Quarry
MOUNT EDGCUMBE
Italian Gardens
The Avenue
Bath Ho.
Mount Edgcumbe Battery
Wilderness Point

W. H. Maddock's
MAP OF
PLYMOUTH, DEVONPORT, STONEHOUSE,
STOKE, MORICE-TOWN, FORD,
-and the Neighbourhood.
Lithographed & Printed by W. H. Maddock, 86, Treville St. Plymouth.
COPYRIGHT 1877
Scale 12 Inches to a Mile
PLYMOUTH
Plymouth, Stonehouse and Devonport Cemetery
Ford Park
DEVON
RAILWAY
SOUTH
MUTLEY STATION
Devonport Prison
Cemetery Road
NORTH ROAD
STATION
Workhouse
SOUTH DEVON HOSPITAL
Alma Villas
Burgoyne Villas
Devonshire Villas
Mill Pond
Orphan's Home
Staddon Ter.
Albert Road
North Road
Portland Villas
PORTLAND SQUARE
Oxford St.
Cambridge St.
Morley St.
King Street
Frankfort Street
Cornwall St.
Park Street
Clarence St.
Duke St.
Regent St.
Mount Pleasant
Friary Station
Sutton Pool
Sutton Harbour Station
Union Street
The Crescent
PRINCESS SQUARE
Princess Street
Millbay Barracks
Millbay Road
Mill Bay
Hoe Park
HOE PROMENADE
THE HOE
CITADEL
Citadel Road
Walker Terrace
West Hoe Road
Radford Road
Grand Parade
Promenade Pier
Rope Walk
Commercial Wharf
Deadmans
Breakwater
Mt BATTEN
Workhouse

Duprez
Camera Obscura, Plymouth Hoe c 1865

PHOTOGRAPHERS IN VICTORIAN PLYMOUTH

The earliest professional photographers were known as Artists or Professors, and John Blake at The Royal Union Baths adjacent to the Railway arch in Union Street who described himself as a Daguerreotype Artist was working in Plymouth as early as 1852, a year later than the first portrait in the Mayor's album. The Daguerreotype process invented in France achieved clearer portraits than the calotype first patented by Henry Fox Talbot, a Westcountryman.

Photographers were prepared to travel to the homes of the gentry "distance of no consequence", and pictures survive of them, their houses, dogs and servants, including butlers with powdered wigs.

These "gems of art" were displayed in Union, George and Bedford Streets, and they inspired Louis Duprez who at the age of twenty-five in 1869, published a booklet of twenty "Photographic views of Plymouth and neighbourhood" and "A Photographic and Parliamentary Album of Devon and Cornwall" for which all the local M.P.s sat specially. He featured advertisements of high class commercial establishments in Plymouth such as the new Duke of Cornwall Hotel, to help cover expenses, and both views and portraits together with those of local clergy, ministers, nobility and gentry could be purchased at sixpence each.

"For brilliancy, clearness and truthfulness, Duprez's photographs stand unrivalled, the light of The Hoe being the only good place for pictures". His West of England Portrait & Landscape Studio was nearby; "exact representations of objects and places cannot fail to be truthful", he claimed. The informal crowd scenes he took during Regatta Week were relegated to the family album because there was movement during the ten minute exposure. The lady sitting outside The Camera Obscura has a strained expression due to the clamp round her neck to help her to keep still long enough; men were able to combat this discomfort by putting on a forceful expression, in Victorian eyes equivalent to dignity. The placard beside her advertises a show by El Hyder, Don Ferreyra and John of Paris, who were no doubt conjurors; the latter may be Duprez himself, Jean Louis Philippe born in 1884 at Barnstable, son of a Frenchman, Monsieur Jean Duprez, Professor of Languages, who moved to Plymouth by 1862. Louis Duprex was well known as a conjuror from c 1870, appearing in London at The Crystal Palace and Egyptian Hall. He finally abandoned photography in 1879, advertising his services as "conjuror, practiser & teacher of sleight of hand" and "Professor of Magic". Later he toured the seaside resorts. His act included "some exceptionally intelligent dogs, Colonel Spot, the Doctor, etc., taught by kindness only". His last engagement was Christmas 1898 at Hastings Pier, where he was taken ill and died in lodgings there the following spring, without returning home to his daughters in Plymouth.

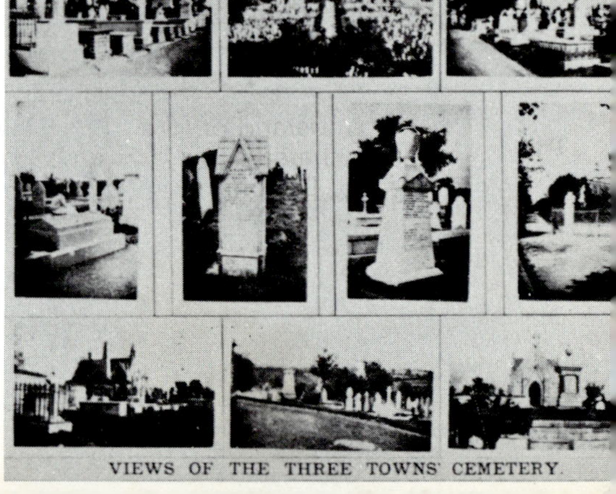

Plymouth, Devonport & Stonehouse cemetery, 1868.

Visitors came to see the memorials ranging from chaste classical urns to elaborate Celtic crosses and Gothic revival, like the earliest monument dated 1848 in memory of a three year old child. Parson Hawker of Morwenstow, who was born and died in Plymouth, was buried here in 1875.

Crocquet match at Penlee Gardens, Stoke, c 1865

The Gardener and his wife. Penlee Gardens c 1865.

William Gage Tweedy of Plymouth wrote, in the March 1863 issue of *The Photographic News* about the revolving camera he had invented, primarily for the use of surveyors, by which a picture could be taken on a flat piece of glass and one continuous view include the sweep of the horizon. However, the Wet Collodion process he used required a wagon load of apparatus, and the camera was more suited to group photography; by 1884, Doidge & Company had the largest Studio in the west of England and could accommodate a party of sixty.

Friese Greene, of Bath had a photographic shop and studio in Plymouth for a short time at 155A Union Street, (The Octagon side of the railway arch, opposite the site of The Royal Union Baths where Plymothians were taking the spa waters at the time that Henry Fox Talbot the first photographer to cross The Tamar, visited Carclew). There were still gardens in Union Street, but the varied entertainments available were becoming well known throughout the west country. As photography became cheaper and more popular in the eighteen eighties competition increased. In 1881 the twenty-six year old Society Photographer wooed the public with verse, "A travelling Companion", and "Little Laughing Rosa" in 1882. Scammel, 3 Bank of England Place in 1885 advertised "The Seven Wonders of Plymouth", and hoped to attract "the jolly Jack Tar" and "the sewing machine maiden". They spent their money on such novelties as hand painted photographic birthday, wedding and Easter cards by Rundle & Codd of Bedford Street, and pictures on opal or porcelain "guaranteed to withstand all the ravages of time, change and the climate" by Hawke of George Street. Later Prior's Stoke Newsagency published a postcard series of the Plymouth & Devonport celebrity pavement entertainers. An obliging Flora Place photographer was prepared to take "absent or deceased friends, at the shortest notice".

Duprez
The bandstand on The Hoe c 1868.
"As animated a view as can be found on the south coast of Devon."

Friese Greene at the time he was experimenting on the cinematograph and filing patents in the 1880's.

A TRAVELLING COMPANION.

One takes a book to while away
The hours upon the Rail;
Another with a stranger chats,
Or listens to his tale.
The doting mother with her babe
Is blest as blest can be;
And thus Time passes, until each
The journey's end doth see.
I with me *my* companion take,
And while on it I look,
I need not with a stranger talk,
Or peep within a book.
Oh! happy as a king am I,
While in my hand is seen
The photo. of the girl I love,
As taken by **FRIEZE GREENE.**

Cartes, 4/- per dozen.

Note the address—155A, *UNION ST., PLYMOUTH.*

Willy Friese Greene was undoubtedly working on his cinematograph whilst at Plymouth. He had put a manager in the business so that he could press ahead with the experiments. James Adams, himself working on a machine camera that subsequently produced a picture two foot square knew him but they didn't go into partnership due to Friese Greene's departure from Plymouth in 1883 to go to London.

A. T. Abrahams was a well known photographer in Plymouth and Devonport who collaborated with Fred Jane, a Havant publican to produce the famous *Jane's Fighting Ships*. The postcards that he published of "great Naval deeds" in the Kaiser's war and the twenty inches by fifteen inches "Grid-iron manoeuvre", brought him fame. His son Jim took his first picture of a Russian bear on H.M.S. *Empress of India* at the age of twelve and went on to make films for the navy. "The Faulkland Islands Battle" and "The Flag Lieutenant" in 1919.

Many designs on the reverse of cabinet photographs are merely ornamental. Major & Darker's staff of cherubs seem to have some technical knowledge . . .

THE WESTERN FIGARO.

My little, laughing Rosa
Doth often to me say—
"Do let me have my Photo, Pa;
You must not say me nay.
You know that I have many a friend,
To whom I shall my Portrait send."

I can resist no longer;
I must my darling please,
And to the Studio of FRIESE GREENE,
Conduct the handsome teaze.
The SPECIMENS I've there beheld
I own I've never seen excell'd.

FRIESE GREENE,

PHOTOGRAPHIC ARTIST,

The Corridor, 155A, *UNION ST., PLYMOUTH.*

4s. per doz. Highest style of Photograph, **10**s. per dozen; and Cabinets, **2**s. the first, and **1**s. each after.

A portrait by John Palmer of Union Street who patented the *"chromocretae photograph"*.

If a soldier or sailor wanted pictures for his girlfriends, nine of Palmer's *"American Gems"* photos cost 7½d.

Godfrey Wycisk and his younger brother John photographed in their Sunday best by W. H. Waterfield of Marlborough Street in 1899. It was an ordeal after the excitement of the tram ride to Devonport, and hard for them to keep still long enough; but a stand was provided as well as the rope to give Godfrey support during the lengthy exposure required.

J. S. Constable

The Photographic Club, Royal Naval Engineering College, Keyham, August 1891; that year the distinctive grouping of buttons on the uniform of the 'engineer students' was abandoned.
This picture was carefully pasted into the album that recorded the club's activities; the college at work, sports day, and trips up the Lynher River, the Tamar and Tavy.

Messrs. Tope (left) and Monk at Mother Hubbard's Cottage, Yealmpton, c 1900.

Rugg Monk poses with his camera beside the band during a river trip. No doubt such songs as "Did you ever see an oyster walk upstairs" would later be sung. His public readings in dialect were popular, and he might be prevailed upon to oblige.

Wild Men of Borneo at Barnum's Circus, Plymouth, c 1900 Rugg Monk
Mrs. Barnum was a South Devon girl, and the circus always received a warm reception. An enthusiastic admirer of their elephant Jumbo sent a bucket of champagne from America, followed the next week by six dozen oysters; a newly married couple even sent a piece of their wedding cake for him.

Waggonette Outing to Holbeton

For the benefit of amateur photographers, W. Ingles Rogers of St. Germans first wrote *"One hundred photographic dodges"*, and followed up with four hundred extra suggestions in *"a casket of photographic gems"* in 1890.

Rugg Monk, a jeweller did much of his own developing. He gave talks on the history of Plymouth and illustrated them by lantern slides; he copied old rare photographs of the city and also took photographs of the districts that were being redeveloped. In his capacity as a Plymouth councillor he took photographs of Burrator reservoir being constructed, while Robert Burnard, another Plymouth businessman was tramping Dartmoor taking photographs in the company of Rev. Sabine Baring Gould.

Rugg Monk

Cyclists at Anthony c 1900.
Notice the bicycle lamps and adjustable wicks. Eastman Kodak at this time had advertised a camera with a roll film, eminently suitable for lady cyclists.

THE HOE c 1860
The Hoe before development was an uneven place where children played at rolling down the hollows. Pensioners spring cleaned carpets there before 9 a.m., beating them with sticks for a charge of half a crown. Sheep, and broken down horses, recuperating before resale, grazed there. Gill's Cottages built beside the quarry housed the navvies working there, who, by the 1850's had removed a large part of West Hoe. The area available for recreation was increased by the levelling of the outer defences of The Citadel in 1888. The Trinity obelisk painted red and white was blown up on 20th October 1882 and replaced by Smeaton's tower, formerly the Eddystone lighthouse.

Drake's Island with its newly-built casemates, The Terrace and nearby baths at West Hoe, c 1870.

Regatta Day 1868
The Citadel, Camera Obscura and flagstaff seen from West Hoe; note the Bath chair in the foreground. By this time the number of Bath chairs lenders in Plymouth and Stonehouse had declined due to the closing of the Royal Union Baths in 1860. Jugglers entertained crowds on such occasions; at the 1882 regatta however, a juggler dressed like a Turkish Dragoman had hardly opened his bag of tricks at West Hoe, when the Police moved him on.

H.M. training brigs Nautilus and Seaflower (attached to H.M.S. Impregnable) moored off Drake's Island, c 1880. Behind H.M.S. *Seaflower* can be seen the Trinity Obelisk and the crenellated building locally known as "Tom thumb's Castle". The site for the promenade pier below the "Bull Ring" can be clearly seen.

The Camera Obscura c 1868, where for one penny Plymouth and The Sound "with all the various shades and colours were enhanced by the contraction of the view provided by a revolving periscope reflected onto a horizontal oval table".
"The semi-nautical and military male gossips of the neighbourhood" congregated here. By the flagpole stands the Hoe Constable. In July 1884, during a fireworks display some boys crept onto the roof. With great presence of mind the lady in charge set the cupola in motion with a suddeness that startled them, and fearing that an earth tremor was starting, they ran away.

The "Bull Ring", c 1868 Duprez

On the "Corporation Seat", now part of The Belvedere, sat the veterans who in their youth had fought at Trafalgar and Waterloo. The "Bull Ring" can be seen below. Here the bulls were tied by a long rope round their horns to a stake, and baited by bulldogs, which were sometimes tossed in the air and their owners would run forward to catch them. On occasions the rope snapped and the bull mad with pain and fury would rush through the town pursued by a mob. When caught, a butcher would cut the back tendons of the bull's legs. Some thought that this made the meat tender, as in the case of a hunted hare; but W. F. Collier, the first M.P. for Plymouth after the 1832 Reform Act, recalled that the flesh tasted feverish and unwholesome. Political meetings were also held here. The last one was on June 7th, 1882 to celebrate the fiftieth anniversary of the passing of the Reform bill.

There was a tram service from Derry's Clock, and many came to see the balloon ascent from The Hoe during Regatta week.

Horse Tram at West Hoe, c 1894.

From right to left, The Esplanade, Elliott Terrace, The Camera Obscura, Duprez's West of England Portrait Studio and Gill's Quarrymen's cottages. The Mayflower Post House and The Berni Grand now dominate the skyline.

West Hoe Terrace and Drake's Island c 1868. Duprez
Sheep graze in the quarry where John Smeaton supervised the shaping of granite blocks for his lighthouse.

Rugg Monk

The Breakwater Lighthouse, c 1900.
This lighthouse keeper was less isolated than most. On a calm day excursionists enjoy a walk here. At mid day a service was held by the Seaman's Mission in the lighthouse. Stone for repairs was at this time unloaded from the *Recovery*, a boat which had an iron winch on board, and the crane by the jetty was seldom used.

The Breakwater Crew in their cutter photographed alongside a Tamar barge loading crushed limestone by the old kilns near Laira Bridge.

The men who worked on the Breakwater were necessarily proficient oarsmen because in bad weather it might take two hours to get there. They took part in the regattas at Plymouth, Stonehouse, North Corner, St. Budeaux and Saltash, often competing against the tattooed muscles of the Navy. They had a proud record of winning fourteen matches out of seventeen, and Arthur James Glinn remembers Coxon Passmore, and ten others of the eleven that pulled with him in 1908; Jackson, Harper, Dare, Thorn, Oxland, Harper (father and son), Hodges, Johns and Brown. It was not unusual for them to pull from Oreston to Looe, race, then return the same evening.

Youth and Old Age
The Hoe, c 1892
3 Elliott Terrace was the Plymouth home of Lady Nancy Astor, M.P. for Plymouth who became in 1919 the first women member of the House of Commons. When it was suggested that her husband should buy a yacht, Nancy replied; "It was the people I wanted to get to know, not the fishes."

Duprez
Plymouth Regatta Day 1869.
The ladies stand on the balcony at The Royal Western Yacht Club. Since the completion of the Breakwater sailing enthusiasts had visited Plymouth. On May 23rd, 1879, W. S. Gilbert arrived on his 63 ton schooner *Pleione.* He visited Looe, and immortalised the fisherman's song "I have a song to sing 'O." The Prince of Wales sailed here with the Lipton family and the first Lord Revelstoke. For the not so wealthy, the Minima Yacht Club on the pier welcomed members.

Duprez
Plymouth Regatta Day 1869.
The Sound was always crowded with foreign vessels, coasters, packets, fishing boats, emigrant boats and other passenger ships; sometimes the Royal Yacht . . .

The Marine Biological Headquarters being constructed in 1887. The excavation of the two storage reservoirs was a major undertaking. Local boys used to meet the aquarium boats, and in return for their help in unloading, gained free entry.

Occasionally there were as many as two hundred Cornish luggers that had come from as far as St. Ives or Penzance at The Barbican. There was a tunnel from The Hoe to The Barbican, and the iron gates were closed at sunset. Late comers to the citadel entered by 'the sally port' nearby.

Smeaton's Tower, c 1892

"Somehow Smeaton's Tower doesn't present a striking appearance on The Hoe; I don't think that it will be anything of an attraction its projectors anticipated, but we shall have to put up with it." The Editor *Western Figaro,* June 1884. Even with its first coat of paint, it can be seen that all the joints are close and uniform. The storm doors were retained as well as a model of the original candle-frame, complete with twenty-four candles, "as curious in its way as 'Puffing Billy' is to railway enthusiasts".

When the monster Diamond Jubilee bonfire was lit on June 22nd, 1897, the officials sitting in the front row were harrassed by the insects that flew out of the timbers which had been taken from condemned houses in Looe Street. It was a day to remember for children too; they were given a medal and a flag, and marched to The Hoe where oranges and large currant buns were distributed.

F. G. Coles

Feu-de-Joie, June 22nd, 1897

The crowds on The Hoe could see rifle smoke rising above the trees at Picklecombe Fort and the batteries around The Sound.

The Citadel, c 1869 Duprez

The dry moat was used for musketry practice and the drawbridge hauled up every night at 10 p.m.

When Major William Gammell who had served in the Peninsular war died at Stonehouse in 1853, a fine memorial depicting the weapons of the day was erected at the new Plymouth, Devonport & Stonehouse Cemetery, (Ford Park). The town still largely relied on the Citadel guns for defence, and shipping in The Sound had to avoid target practice from The Lower Battery. The ring of "Palmerston forts", built primarily to protect the naval base completely encircled the town by the early eighteen sixties. Civilians were encouraged to participate in home defence and the second Devon Rifle Volunteers were then based at the Charity School in Catherine Street. The Royal Naval Artillery Volunteers first met at 7.30 p.m., September 9th, 1881 in The Corinthian Yacht Club below The Citadel. Robert Burnard, a Plymouth businessman presided. Until disbanded ten years later, they drilled, practised their rifle and cutlass exercises at Devil's Point. Plymothians were always aware that this is a garrison town. In July 1883 a spectator wrote "the evolutions of the Highland Infantry" on The Hoe caused a stir. "The brave fellows make a bayonet charge at nothing at all with a wild cheer. One can fancy a little bit what the real thing must be."

Carriages at Citadel Road, c 1892
The old houses in St. Andrew's Street and Spooner's Corner can be clearly seen. At premises near the Georgian synagogue (adjacent to the Treasury Building), the photographer A. T. Abrahams arranged the reception of Jews who had arrived in Plymouth by boat from The Pogroms, and their subsequent rail journey to different parts of The British Isles.

A study of hobnail boots and an Indian Ayah.
Windsor Terrace, c 1900.
Rugg Monk
The nursemaids no doubt were employed by military families.

Rugg Monk
Citadel Road, c 1900
The Holiday Inn now dominates the skyline.
Sheep graze where approximately sixty thousand people witnessed the unveiling of the Armada monument in 1890. Redcoats lined the route from the Guildhall Square via Bedford Street, George Street and Lockyer Street to the enclosure. It was impossible not to feel a glow of patriotism when drums were beating and trumpets sounding, and the music of navy army and Volunteer bands was to be heard. The only disappointment was that Queen Victoria forbade the sending of a gunboat or that the training brigs be dressed overall because nothing should be done to offend Spain.

The Auditorium, Plymouth Pier, c 1889
"The whirl of gaieties" presented at the Promenade Pier, the Theatre Royal, or Palace of Varieties, the excitement involved in the parade of troops at the Raglan barracks and reviews of the Naval Brigade on the Brickfields at Devonport, a ride from Derry's Clock in an electric tram, made Plymouth in 1900 "the terrestial paradise of the modern excursionist . . . Everything that can mitigate the little ills of life and increase the joys of mere living" was available here.

The Pier, c 1897, where sitting on the seats with Dolphin arms it was possible to listen to the band and watch the ironclads being towed out into The Sound.

At specified times, as indicated by the four illuminated dials of the Pier Clock, bands played waltz music at the pavilion, where for sixpence a pair of roller skates could be hired. Eighteen lamps of two thousand candle power helped to draw the crowds here for boxing on Sunday evenings. Other entertainments included fishing competitions, and an acrobat occasionally performed on the end of a greasy pole; nothing to rival Blondin who had made three journeys on a tight rope fifty feet up near The Citadel, with a bandage over his eyes in 1862.

S.S. *Alexandra* at the Pier steamer berth,

Steps that rang with the sound of hobnail boots on metal as children rushed off the boat. Steamers belonging to The Plymouth Pier & Steamboat Company "plied to quaintest hamlets on the Cornish coast famed for their breed of hardy fishermen and with histories of smuggling or worse. Alternatively to the Devon watering places sacred to the elite; the home of palatial yachts that cruise on the summer seas".

Plymouth Promenade Pier & Pavilion

THE FINEST PIER PAVILION IN ENLGAND.

FRESH WATER DOUCHE AND DIVING PLATFORM FOR BATHERS.

Promenade Concerts every Sunday Evening.

Besides the Deck of the Pier there is a Grand Balcony Promenade.

MILITARY BANDS, CONCERTS, AND SPECIAL ENTERTAINMENTS DAILY,

At 3-15 p.m. and 8 p.m. throughout the season. PIER TOLL, 2d.

Pleasure Steamers constantly leaving the Pier for the FIVE beautiful rivers in the neighbourhood, Sea Trips and surrounding places of interest.

JOHN HIGSON, Manager.

Plymouth Pier was opened on 29th May, 1884 at a cost of £45,000. Five years later, five thousand one pound shares were sold to enable the auditorium to be covered in. For the Royal Plymouth Corinthian Yacht Club matches "two brass cannon were mounted on the end of the pier; their polished muzzles looking out towards The Sound as though capable of keeping a whole Armada at bay."

The Refreshment Stall on The Pier. Afternoon tea was served in the restaurant.

At specified times, as indicated by the four illuminated dials of the Pier Clock, bands played waltz music at the pavilion, where for sixpence a pair of roller skates could be hired. Eighteen lamps of two thousand candle power helped to draw the crowds here for boxing on Sunday evenings. Other entertainments included fishing competitions, and an acrobat occasionally performed on the end of a greasy pole; nothing to rival Blondin who had made three journeys on a tight rope fifty feet up near The Citadel, with a bandage over his eyes in 1862.

Message on the reverse:
"I'm in the pink of health at present."
Cysieus Publishing Co., Fife

"Hokey Pokey a penny a lump, taste before you buy".
The Italian ice cream vendor was kept so busy that he didn't have time to change the washing-up water for his halfpenny glasses. Nearby a man cut out silhouettes of children clutching their buckets and spades.

Plymouth Pier, c 1892 W. H. Waterfield
Watermen stand by the steps leading to the Ladies' Bathing Place.

The Western Figaro satirist occasionally noticed that disasters were caused by the watermen who tarred the seats of their boats which were for hire adjacent to the pier. The passengers found that once aboard it was "U.P. with your spicey pants, or with fair Florrie's pale blue Indian cloud costume." Nearby a notice concerning the Ladies' Bathing Place read: "Gentlemen are requested to keep to the higher walks between the hours of ten and twelve."

Refreshment Stall at The Belvedere, 1897.

"A City with lots of lights and fairs."
(*Cornish Waif's Story*)

Part of the celebrations for Queen Victoria's Diamond Jubilee, 1897, at West Hoe.

Bathers on The Pier, 1897.
At Regatta time the "Seven o'clock Regulars" the "Shackey Pool Stragglers" and "the Tinside Champions", all rival clubs, joined in "bathing comradeship". A highlight was the theme of tall white sugar loaf hats with the legend that read "we are the Seven o'clock Regulars" as they bobbed about in the water.

"I am very glad to hear that the wearing of bathing drawers is becoming more and more popular every day with the bathers." (Editor *Western Figaro*, June 25th, 1886). Nevertheless men still dived off the Pier naked in the 'Nineties.

"Lionel and his school-fellows." A detail from a photograph by Albert P. Steer, at The Hoe Preparatory School, Summer 1903.

Duprez

Crescent Place, Mulgrave Street looking towards Lockyer Street, 1868
The photographer's home was at number two ; next door, was Mrs. Lane's boarding School. She and other schools in the district advertised in the local papers for pupils each summer.

Boy with a peg leg.
Athenaeum Street, c 1868. Duprez
In the distance behind Henry Matthews' baker's cart, are The Crescent Gardens.

The corner of Lockyer Street and Citadel Road, c 1868. Duprez
At Windsor Terrace (left) where now Armada Way links the City Centre and The Hoe, Robert White Stevens, correspondent of *The Times* at Plymouth, often paused at dinner with his family to listen to the firing of guns which told the tonnage of incoming vessels.

Charabanc party outside The Royal Hotel. Notice the solid tyres. There were difficulties in drawing over the concertina hood.
The earliest motor coach in Plymouth, "Norah", owned by Mr. Hill a cafe proprietor in Union Street took two days to make the round trip to Barnstaple. In 1919 Turner's 28 seat Karrier's fuel consumption was six miles to the gallon.

St. Catherine's, Lockyer Street designed by John Foulston. Formerly it also had a bell tower, like that at Dulwich Art Gallery designed by Sir John Soane. As at the Theatre Royal, cast iron pillars were used. The Dartmoor granite facade was a contrast to the few remaining stucco buildings of his Regency town centre that remain until its demolition in January 1958.

Lockyer Street Lodge, c 1868. Duprez
The Hoe Park Constable lived here.

'The Devon & Cornwall Female orphanage Asylum, formerly in Lockyer Street, was built in 1842. The children's uniform was a sharp contrast to those more fortunate who attended preparatory schools in the district. This was a restrained building for the usually flamboyant George Wightwick.

Lockyer Street looking towards Bank of England Place, c 1896.
The Royal Hotel site and St. Catherine's, right, are now car parks.

The interior showing a painting over the altar by the Plymouth artist Benjamin Haydon, who painted some of his most famous canvases in a debtor's prison.

Electric trams at the points in Bank of England Place, looking towards The Royal Hotel and Lockyer Street, c 1908.
The manager of the Plymouth branch of the Bank of England (right) lived in style at the Bank House, with liveried footmen.
As a boy in the eighteen sixties, James Rendel Harris, the Paeleontologist who translated the *Codex Sinaiticus*, played cricket on the stairs of his parents' house nearby at 197 Union Street where they lived over their business (picture dealers, painters, decorators). On one occasion running after the ball, he fell down an open coal hole. These were the days when children were taken to the tailors twice a year to have clothes made to measure. "The *Practical Tailor*" at The Army & Navy Outfitters of Union Street in 1882 advertised Ladies & Gentlemen's chest expanding braces that could be "worn without inconvenience, a positive comfort to the wearer" . . .

UNION STREET from the railway arch looking towards Bank of England Place. On the left is the site of Western Approach and Devonshire Terrace where Doidge's Annual was published.
"Gatti, chocolate bon-bons and French bread" and "menus such as one is accustomed to find at the best places on The Strand", were to be found at Ferrari's Swiss cafe. This "parade for Plymothians" provided a good range of shops, theatres and other diversions. While William Sweet's Naval and masonic outfitters could supply 45/- tailor-made serge suits and his specialite for the man about town in the 1880's was an indigo beaver overcoat at 35/-. Tipsy sailors chose to have a more permanent memento of Plymouth and bared their chests etc. at the studio of the master tattoist.
Certain pubs were patronised by Naval officers. *The Birkhead Hotel* near the railway arch advertised that the landlord, Tom Johnson, gave a genial welcome; more important, his was a full measure. Businessmen, whose homes were in Union Street, and commercial travellers came there for "hot scotch and a perusal of the papers for three D." Their wives were not molested when they walked up the street towards the Halfpenny Bridge at Stonehouse if they walked on the right hand pavement. It it was wet underfoot they had to hold up their trailing skirts with one hand.
On Saturday evenings the Navy Patrol were out in force and policemen would rap the deserted tram lines with their "night sticks" if they required assistance. Violence in the pubs, even the occasional stabbing was expected. In December 1904, P.C. 19 was cautioned by the Plymouth Watch Committee for assaulting a prostitute. Relations with the police were more amicable, and the girls helped with enquiries about wanted men and goods smuggled off foreign ships. They were left alone to walk the streets where "the lamps lit by naked gas jets glistened as the damp wooden blocks of the road reflected the light". In a seamist, the Thameside exploits of Sherlock Holmes could easily have taken place in Union Street, and in fact Conan Doyle knew "The Three Towns" when he was for a short time assistant to Dr. Budd.

Behind the tram, at 198 Union Street was the Plymouth Dairy Company, where cups of milk with Devonshire cream, milk and soda, koumiss and plates of junket were popular with shoppers. Customers could inspect the kitchen; a showpiece with Golden cream cooling in fifty gleaming brass pans on iron stands. A fernery in the back yard completed the impression of a country dairy. Boys were recommended to come here rather than roam the streets smoking cheap cigars in the evenings. Later the premises became Williams cafe, which offered a choice of "piquant pleasantries and ten daintily prepared sweets."

Crescent Avenue, The Hoe, in the early 'Twenties.
Guy Prance's "Radio Car" (note the height of the two aerials. He built a two kilowatt transmitter at his home in Holyrood Place before the B.B.C. broadcast from Athenaeum Lane). This "showman engineer", as an advertisement for The Hippodrome, had the chassis on a Ford car reversed and driven round the Hoe at twenty m.p.h.

Bank of England Place, c 1900.
A roadsweeper's barrow by the portico of The Royal Hotel.

UNION STREET, c 1932.

At The Posada, famed for Buchanan blend whisky, as supplied to the House of Commons, there was a brisk counter trade in wines bottled in the cellar by a machine with a half a dozen syphons that dealt with a hogs head in forty-five minutes without spilling a drop. The Naval officers appreciated the freshly made crayfish sandwiches washed down with a good pint of beer from the wood. Opposite at Wright's hair-dressing saloons, old gentlemen who could remember the hairstyles of Regency Plymouth, in the 1880's were confronted by American shaving chairs and hair brushing by hydraulic power.

UNION STREET, The Railway Arch. On the left is *The Birkhead Hotel.* A large performing bear, muzzled but not caged, and a man on whose shoulders sat a parrot picking out playing cards so that fortunes could be told, were occasionally seen here at the turn of the century. "Pennycross Bill", wearing paper leggings and sand shoes could be seen rubbing his back against the wall. His attempts at playing the mouth organ were not as appreciated as the cart wheels he turned to entertain the children at 1d. a time. He was a familiar figure to them as he walked for miles carrying his teacan. He was welcome at Sunday School outings. His family disowned him, although he never harmed anybody. During a funeral at St. Peter's, Wyndham Square, he shuffled into the church and placed a bunch of violets on the Vicar's coffin, turned and went out. He and the woman who sang "the roses around the door" accompanied by her blind husband who wore a faded green coat, could hold out their tin cups and be certain of a response.

Celebrities.] "OH: BE CAREFUL——" [No.2.—"Pennycross Bill,

"Jack Tar" had spent most of his money by the time he had visited the cast iron urinal in Bath Street (near the arch) to "shed a tear for Nelson", but then, hoping that his entertainment for the night was not over, he bought lavender bags or "sweet violets, sweet violets, a penny a bunch" from "Lavender Lil" nearby.

Over the years a number of entertainers were associated with Union Street. Dusty Brown, the red-haired sword swallower took a swig of meths before he rose to stick sewing needles in the folds of his ribs or tilted his head back to lower a poker down his throat. After sufficient "encouragement" had been placed in the cap at his feet, he swallowed a watch. Clutching the chain between his teeth, he challenged his audience to listen to it "ticking in the depths of the 'uman stummick', ladies and gentlemen".

Like him, the "one man band", (clapper on head, drum on back and cymbals), " I can't sing two songs at once" and the banjomen sometimes provided as much amusement as the music hall artistes.

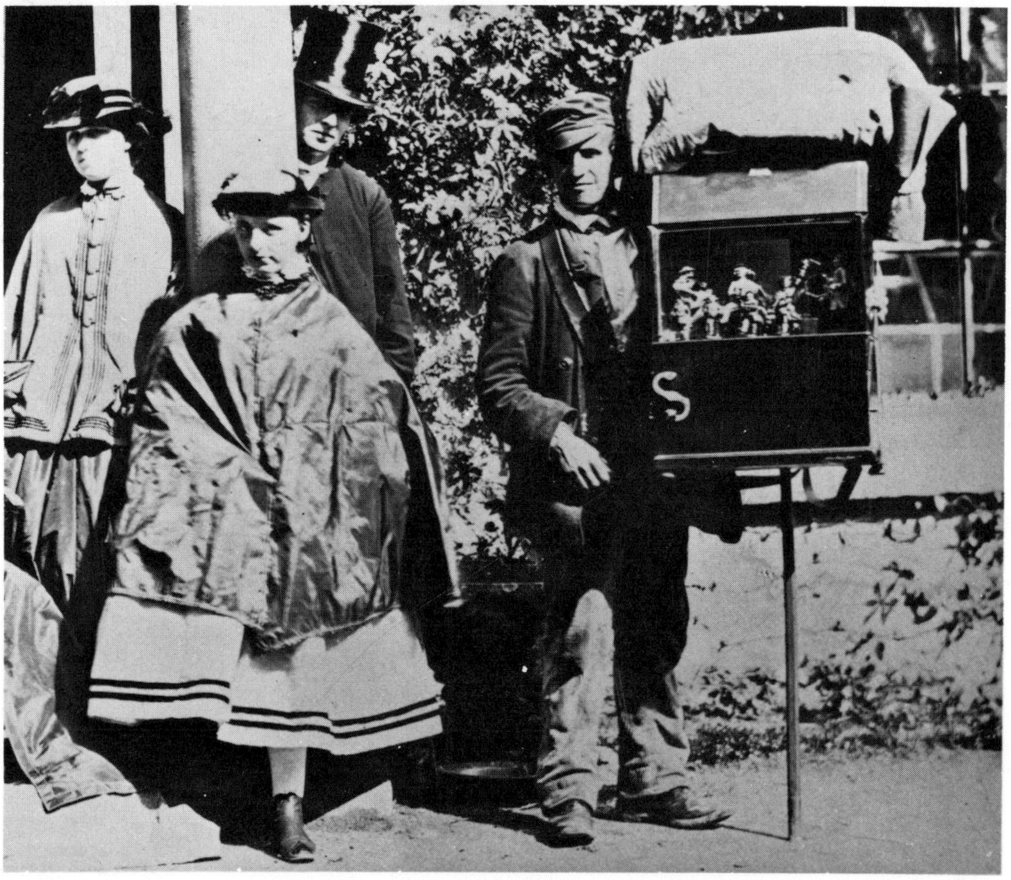

"The dark and sad-eyed Italians twirl the handle of the "jingle-box" or "hurdy-gurdy", grinding out a familiar tinny tune at the same tempo."

A man on stilts publicising the forthcoming events at the fair would in the morning tap on all the tenement windows in King Street. He was a freelance, and relied on contributions for his "lodgings bag".

KING STREET

Mr. Pratt the organ grinder, his wife and Bruce the monkey, the latter a familiar sight with his red cap and jacket lived in a single room there. Every night Mrs. Pratt prepared the same supper of fried cheese and bacon pieces. Seemingly they never purchased any fish from the women whose carts clustered around the railway arch, or sampled hot udder that tasted like chicken. The monkey, whose antics were watched by a small but attentive audience, feasted on chipped potatoes that the Italians sold in the evenings after visiting most parts of the city with their ice cream carts during the day. Barrel organs were hired out in Queen Street nearby. For Bucchini, (locally known as Buggianna) Plymouth's last known organ grinder the new King Street must have seemed dull by comparison. At ten o'clock on a Saturday night when the butchers auctioned meat, the rabbit catcher wearing leggings could be seen amongst the crowd with four or five rabbits on his arm; these he would skin on the spot for the buyer.

King Street seen from the corner of Raleigh Street. At the *Barley Sheaf*, scrumpy, as powerful as that the farmers sold in stone bottles at the back of the market, took the varnish off the bar counter.

From a niche where he had been stationed to sell boot and shoelaces that dangled from his left arm, whilst with his right hand he held out a cup, the tall erect figure of a blind Cornish miner wearing a tin notice around his neck exchanged comments with the stall holders across the road; "a dear pathetic figure", the memory of whom made his grand-daughter feel that she wanted to weep, even years later when she wrote *"A Cornish Waif's story"*. She also remembered her bug-infested shakedown, the shared lavatory in the back yard that smelt "beery and horrible" and the sound of street fights at night when a drunken neighbour could be heard lurching up the stairs to present his wife with one or even two black eyes with which she would defiantly face the world the following morning. In spite of the drinking they and friends would club together to find the money to pay for the services of "the large black glass coach with plumes on the four corners" and avoid a pauper's funeral.

TAVERNS VERSUS TEMPERANCE

"No drink or firewater to be sold to Indians". Pubs had this notice in their windows when *"Buffalo Bill"* visited Plymouth in 1903 with his company who were seen standing on street corners blanketted, feathered and silent.

Inside the pubs where heavy Waterford porter cost twopence a pint, there was a variety of entertainment. Sequah, (alias the quack) of Worthey Son & Sequah, a Union Street herbalist arranged his "specimens" in sweet jars on the top of a "penny in the slot piano". He had a coloured chart of a man with "all his inside works" to which he pointed with his wand and indicated what ills could respond to his treatment. After taking his remedies he guaranteed that the recipients could bend bars of iron two inches thick. Pasties were brought round by an old man called "Boadicea" who claimed that he was "a bit of an authority on Roman history". Sammy Onions could be seen stirring pickled onion into his beer; over several pairs of trousers he wore contrasting shorts. This extra insulation was a wise precaution, because on winter evenings the pubs were visited by a musician who kept his foot in the door until he could be persuaded to stop playing his violin.

Song of the street car

Ram 'em in, jam 'em in, push 'em in,
pack, hustle 'em, jostle 'em, poke 'em
in the back, tramp on 'em, stamp
on 'em make their bones crack.
Fat women, slat women, Tom, Dick and
Jack hang on and cling on by tooth
or by hair. Hey there . . . Now stay
there and Pass up your fare.
Western Figaro, January 8th, 1886.

The actor James Doel advertised "genuine wine and spirits, splendid fine flavoured ales to be had as a refresher at the new laughable comedy at the *Coronation Inn*, The Octagon", in 1855.

Horse tram approaching The Octagon.
It was not unusual for men from rival barracks to jump fifteen feet from the top of a tram to be first at the bar. This ditty describes the atmosphere at the time:

When the crew of a destroyer visited St. James' Bar they brought with them Jack, a curly haired retriever who had been given to them by the landlord. After his death he became more famous as "Waterloo Jack" a collecting box for the Red Cross. This was the only licensed picture palace, and had an attractive entrance with verandah portico, and a photographer's shop, the "Stickyback Studio" incorporated. Saturday night at "St. Jimmy's" was a highlight of Union Street life. Many of the landlords were well known people in the city. "The highly respected host of the *Prince George Hotel,* Stonehouse", James Doel, the oldest actor in England, featured in *"The Plymouth Comet"* which included the revered figures of Lady Astor and Henry Whitfeld the journalist.. "Jimmy" sat inside the bar where he had a collection of his stage career mementoes, wearing make-up and a black wig. On being informed that the ships had arrived in The Sound from Autumn Naval manoeuvres he instructed the women present to "Lift up your skirts girls, the fleet's in". At the *West India Pub*, sailors brought in items for the museum which included a stuffed crocodile hanging over the bar, four squirrels playing cards, a particularly fine example of the taxidermist's art along with some stuffed pygmies that didn't require close scrutiny. There were beer barrels to sit on whilst watching a girl strip. The word 'cabaret' was not used first in Union Street; the credit must go to The Royal Corinthian Yacht Club. It was an ambition for most drinkers to work their way through all the pubs in one evening. After their attempts to do this on a Saturday evening, the Plymouth Police pushed them back over the town boundary at Manor Street into the hands of the "Stonehouse babes", those specially selected policemen who were tall and strong enough to deal with offenders from the old Leinster militia who whilst on their six week summer camp at Staddon Heights during the hay and corn harvests, who came to Union Street to quench their thirst on Friday which was paynight. Soon drunk, they were frogmarched face down to the Stonehouse Police Station; if they gave trouble, their noses would be bumped until their protests subsided. Female habitual inebriates were sent by the justices to The Lancashire Inebriates' Reformatory near Blackburn at a cost of half a guinea per week, or to The Irish Roman Catholic St. Patrick's Home for Females, Waterford for half the price. Families of navvies visited by Susan Moon of the Plymouth Mission, whose chapel was at Willow Street, after they had accepted religious tracts were given beef tea and jellies if their need for sustenance was proved. Meadowcroft, a Union Street draper was a keen adherent of temperance. He even drank water in front of his employees.

Tram drivers were always certain of a good cup of tea at Drower's Welcome at The Octagon. The shop front and lamp standard still remain. On the Martin Street wall there is an advertisement for a now vanished firm of drapers. Joseph Boyd Love sold Irish linen, prospered and subsequently purchased Outlands, the home of Captain Scott's family who were brewers. The shops in Plymouth and Devonport were known as "Love's emporiums".

"Incorrodible teeth available to all classes.' A dentist at The Octagon, 1865.

WITHOUT TEETH. WITH TEETH.

To the Nobility, Gentry, and the Public of the Three Towns and its vicinity.
In consequence of numerous applications

MR. R. JORDAN,
SURGEON DENTIST,
15, OCTAGON, UNION ROAD, PLYMOUTH,

Has been induced to open an establishment permanently at No. 15, Octagon, and owing to the improvements in the mechanical department of making teeth, he is enabled to produce the best Stone Incorrodible Teeth available to all classes, his price being **Five Shillings** for each tooth, or in the same ratio for whole or partial sets, warranted to last a person's lifetime, without springs or ligatures, resembling the exact shape and colour as the natural ones. Nothing can increase the price but the quality of the mounting, and in no instance will teeth be supplied without giving entire satisfaction.

Mr. Jordan employs none but accomplished workmen.

Scurvy in the Gums removed in conjunction with the Anidine Tincture.

Loose teeth fastened, whether from age, the use of calomel, or any other cause.

Tartar and all Scorbutic impurities of the teeth removed, and brought to a beautiful pearly white colour.

DECAYED TEETH

Filled up without heat, pain, or pressure, by the invaluable liquid enamel, a white stopping, solely invented and patented by R. Jordan, forming a whole tooth out of a stump, and rendering the teeth secure for mastication!

Parents cannot be too particular in the regulation of Children's Teeth. Mr. Jordan will give his best advice onthe above subject. Schools and Families attended at their own residences by giving a day's notice. Toothache cured, and all operations in Dental Surgery performed.

Hours of attendance from 10 *till* 4, *and from* 5 *to* 7 *in the evening.*

15, OCTAGON, UNION ROAD, PLYMOUTH.

Union Street, c 1868. Duprez

Friese Green later had his studio on the left, adjacent to the railway arch. J. Carvalho's advertisement for "The Little Wonder" refers to the noted cheap house for boots and shoes in Russell Street where gentlemen's sewn and rivetted boots cost eight and sixpence. Real kid ladies' shoes cost four and eleven. The houses in Flora Place with their fine cast iron railings were formerly part of Foulston's grand town plan. One of the villas survives as Oddfellow's Hall.

"In the summer heat the wooden blocks of the road oozed with tar."

The pioneer days of the cinema were perilous ones. The heat of one reel of film being run into a basket and promptly being pushed away to rewind was a major fire risk in St. James' Hall which could seat twelve hundred. The first talkie was there in 1913, and the services of the effects man in the balcony surrounded by tins of peas, coconut shells, bells, motor horns, "thunder sheets" and a wind machine were soon no longer required. Messrs. Coombes' "Living Pictures" may have been the first films seen in Plymouth when a fight between a chimney sweep and a miller took place. In 1906, James Adams, a friend of Friese Greene filmed a comedy in Manor Street where two policemen, one tall, one short dragged children from a basement window and hosed them. In 1923 Guy Prance filmed the Pram Derby which he had helped to start, bricks were used instead of babies; he also filmed the first air mail on its way to London. His news reels were well known outside Plymouth.

Andrew's Picture House, c 1914-18.

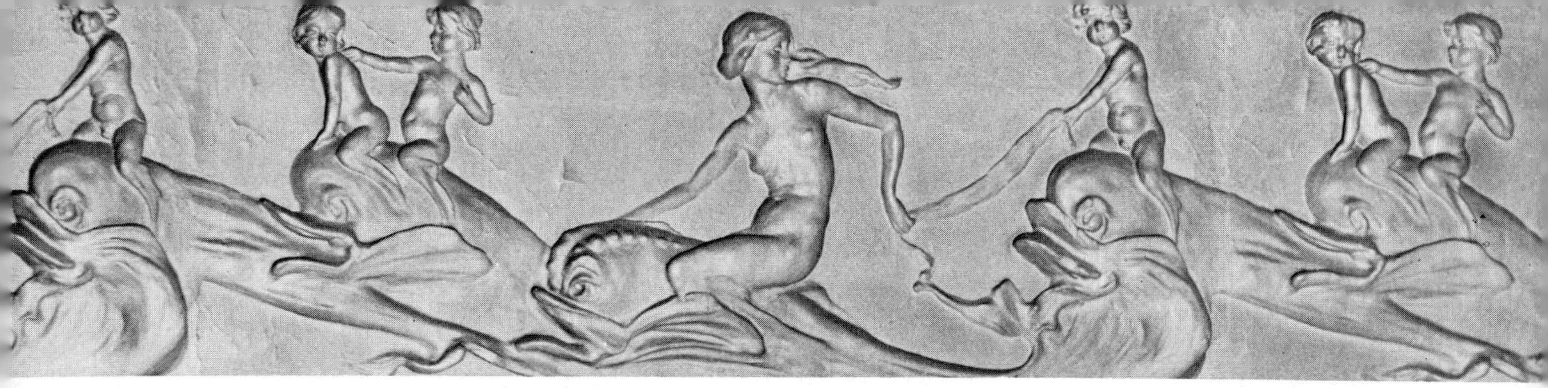

A decorative frieze by Italian craftsmen in the foyer at The **Palace Theatre** where on Monday some families had standing orders for seats in the front row of the stalls, the first night of a new show when the critics were present. A highlight was the entry of Mr. Hoyle wearing a black cape with a scarlet lining over his dress suit. His Rolls Royce is said to have been crimson, and the chauffeur wore a matching uniform. Plymothians have a special affection for the Palace, a few were voluntarily mesmerised, and put in a coffin, but they woke up during another show.

The Grand Theatre, by H. J. Snell a Plymouth architect and the adjoining Grand Theatre Hotel.

The Grand (re) opening of **The Palace**, "The family theatre" under the proprietorship of Thomas Hoyle, September 25th, 1911. Fred Karno's troupe is billed in a poster behind the staff; Charley Chaplin appeared with them in this show.

"Talking pictures" were keen competitors with the live theatre, and after forty-one years "**The Grand**" where a range of entertainers from The D'Oyly Carte Company to the bands of the training ships H.M.S. *Lion* and *Impregnable* appeared, was used as a cinema. With regard to the soundtrack the first words spoken on the stage in 1889 could be interpretted anew: "You little imps what's all this row and riot, I'll knock your heads if you don't keep quiet".

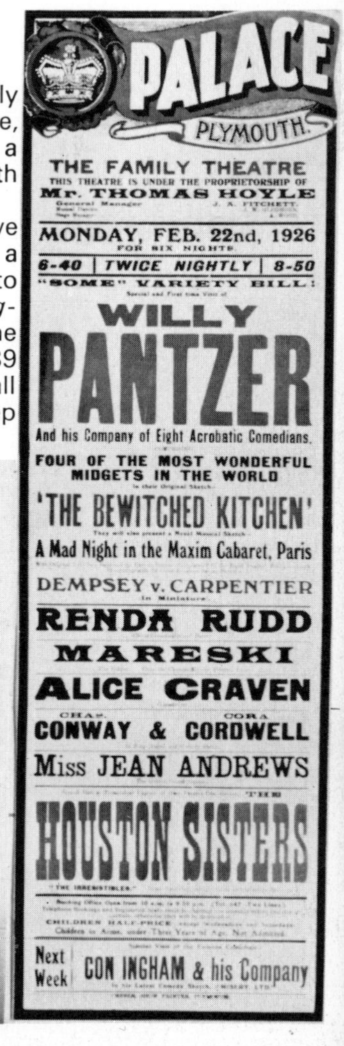

Horse Parade, 1896.
The procession of coal, milk, beer, road-hauliers and fishcarts crosses the tram line leading to Manor Street. The horses and carts were prepared long before the event. The harness after its treatment of being put in a bran bag and pulled up and down looked like burnished silver. Every contestant was proud of his horse with specially plaited straw ribbons in their manes and tails. Opposite is *The Shades* pub that shortly afterwards made way for the *Great Western Hotel* and the famous Long Bar.

Union Street looking towards The Octagon, c 1892. Francis Frith
A fire was kept burning in the cooling room of John Wallington's Turkish Baths at Flora Place. In 1886 a new furnace was installed and purer air was obtained. This service had previously been offered by the Royal Union Baths nearby, which in addition had a saline chalybeate medicinal spring until the building was demolished c 1860. In the entrance to Mr. Bond's veterinary surgery, also in Flora Place, stood a stuffed zebra. Every morning accompanied by his two dalmatians Mr. Bond inspected the two horse trap that had been brought to the front door by two men wearing red coats, white trousers and black boots. After the harness had been inspected, the horses proceeded to high-step down the street with Mr. Bond in brown bowler hat, brown suit and leggings riding in style.

A portrait of a Plymouth beauty photographed by the light of inverted gas mantles at "The Stickyback Studio" adjacent to St. James' Hall. Cut price photography was a competitive business in Union Street, and despite Senior's Photos to "drop in and get snapped", their shop soon closed.

Union Street looking towards Manor Street, December 1908. During the Christmas week trams had to stop in the evenings when crowds tried to erase the lettering that the first "automaticue slide machine" projected on the the road outside St. James' Hall announcing forthcoming events, including a show on the afternoon and evening of Christmas day.

Amongst the crowd at The Octagon on Saturday night could be seen the fishermen on their way to a variety show at either The Grand Theatre, St. James' Hall, the New Palace Theatre, and the short-lived Antelope Music Hall. Gypsies and Italian women with their coloured scarves could be seen near Wallser's Shooting Gallery and Waxworks. Mr. Wallser was in attendance there, wearing a long grey frock coat, a square box hat and smoked a large cigar which he removed from his lips with a flourish. Despite the smell of the waxworks, plenty patronised the penny flea show downstairs. At Teddy Weeks' the opposite side of The Octagon, Saccho the fasting man could be seen in a glass case washing himself with soda water. During the forty days that he was there, the doorman who "had a long sad face with a perpetual dew drop on his nose" kept looking at the small boys who tried to steal a free glimpse round the side of the curtain.

There were a number of stables in the vicinity of Union Street. The arches at Bath Street housed the G.W.R. horses and those belonging to the Three Towns Dairy. Waggonettes and dogcarts were hired out at Octagon Street. The corporation tram stables were here, and were later used by John Hitchings who hired teams of eight horses to the Dockyard. One was provided for the use of the Naval Barracks, and a "Bluejacket" with a dogcart was a familiar sight.

There were two cab ranks at The Octagon. "Jubilee Bill" occasionally entertained people there by talking to the cab horses. One nodded its head and made throaty noises in response to his questions. When a crowd had gathered, Bill promptly came round with the cap.

MILLBAY DOCKS
(North Quay, inner basin) looking towards the Roman Catholic cathedral and the old St. Peter's, Wyndham Square, c 1860.
Stonehouse Hill Fort and its limestone cliff were completely erased.

MILLBAY DOCKS
(East Quay looking towards the Outer Basin and the residence of the King's Harbour Master, c 1868. Duprez

At the height of the passenger ship days nearly a hundred ocean liners docked every month. In the 1890's The Orient Line Steamers dealt with as many as four thousand passengers in a year. The New Zealand Steamship company called both homeward and outward bound, and the Cornish miners travelled between The Cape and this port. In the Millbay Docks at this time one man whilst unloading icing sugar might carry up to $2\frac{3}{4}$ cwt.; backs were rubbed raw if no protective clothing was worn.

Millbay Station, c 1898 Rugg Monk

Millbay Station was opened April 2nd, 1849 and Brunel was present at the "dejeuner a la fourchette" at The Royal Hotel after the ceremony. Nearby was the Patent aerated water company in Station Road, the sole manufacturers of "The summer and the Three Towns Punch". The works was open for inspection every Tuesday. Most varieties of mineral and aerated waters were to be seen there in corked and patent stoppered bottles. An old match seller on crutches was usually outside here when the workers went home in the evenings.

FOOD

Many of the Union Street residents sampled the horse chestnuts and the potatoes in their jackets (four for a penny) on sale here. Diodatto Mignanelli sold chips during the evening and invited Italian Americans back home for spaghetti. Sweetbreads and slices off Algar's hot baron of beef were considered to be a luxury. The counter at *The Farley Hotel* sold fresh sandwiches made to the specification of the customer, and liberally spread with relish and sauces. Ted Week's "Cough no more" boiled sweets flavoured with mint and honey, aniseed and cinnamon were popular. The strawberry candies were made in his shop window at The Octagon. Nearby Sheppard's fourpenny Supper Shop offered faggots and peas, and the Salvation Army dispensed pea soup to the poor. At the Soup kitchen off Flora street, latecomers had the thickest soup with lumps of meat for a penny. Penny pasties were also sold there.

Flora Street decorated for The Diamond Jubilee, 1897.
Rugg Monk

This photograph was taken to show how even the side streets were decorated in honour of the Queen. The Pearse family who lived in the corner house where now The Odeon stands were the first to own a motor car in Union Street. However the milkman standing outside the wine merchants still had to haul the churn by the long wooden handle up the hill holding his stomach unless a helping tow was given by a cart; the brass topped churn was in very hot weather covered with a sun hat. Navvies who lived nearby were a familiar sight in their working clothes that in 1869 consisted of "a blue cap with a polished leather peak, a black silk kerchief tied in a sailor's knot, a white linen smock or 'slop' with herring-bone 'flash' needle work over a double breasted waistcoat of blue plush with large pearl buttons and moleskin sleeves for work in winter; they wore white breeches, blue stockings and ankle boots with 'Van Dyke' stitchings." (William Hirst, *Transactions of the Plymouth Institution* 1899). Thirty years later, fashion had changed the Sunday clothes which then consisted of a dark blue or black coat and corduroy trousers. Hair was carefully plastered down in a 'curlup' on the forehead.

The Mileage Yard Millbay Docks, c 1868. Duprez

Before 1873 all the haulage of trucks at the docks was done by horses. Nearby was the Millbay Soapworks where 15 cwt. barrels of tallow were rolled into the yard. The yellow soap made here has been described as "a legend of the West Country that has found its way to all parts of the world". The Rev. George Berry of Emmanuel Church, Compton even used it to make a model of "New Jerusalem" when raising funds in 1894. Working conditions were hazardous; one man fell into the seventeen foot deep copper in the boiling room. After the tallow had boiled for ten days, all that was left of him were a few brass buttons.

c 1868. Duprez

The County Borough of Stonehouse Fire Brigade, c 1900.

Who could be seen wearing their polished brass helmets, clinging to the horse-drawn fire engine as they sped towards the fire. In this photograph they are standing outside the fire station with their monogrammed sandbags. If there was a large conflagration, the massed fire brigades of the "Three Towns" were not able to assist as well as they might have, due to the different makes of firefighting equipment that they used.

Nearby in West Hoe Road were The Millbay Rinkeries, popular for wrestling and boxing tournaments. At Ballard's Institute schoolboys received sixpence for an evening attendance; "Archie" Ballard rewarded them further if they excelled at P.T.

The London train awaits the foreign mail at East Quay, Millbay Docks. Special correspondents at one time gathered here from all parts of the country awaiting the return of the tender from the Ocean Mail steamer in The Sound with important despatches. Behind the Customs House is Millbay Drill Hall, built on the cantilever principle by The Volunteers in 1870. Before it was blitzed it was used for trade exhibitions and circuses; it could hold six thousand people and in 1891, Gladstone, then "the grand old man" addressed a political meeting there.

A poster for the Italian Circus on the gate of Millbay Barracks. Rugg Monk

Millbay Barracks 1897. Rugg Monk
Prisoners of war were formerly incarcerated here. The gallows were set up in 1807 for the last time in Plymouth on waste ground outside the barracks when a Spanish prisoner was hung for stabbing a man who denied him bread and cheese.

The pungent smell of hot horse dung at the cab rank in George Street, c 1898. The tram shelter and George Street before the introduction of the electric trams. Nearby the cry of the shoe black boy "clean your shoes Sir" could be heard in the vicinity of The Theatre Royal portico.

Young children were told by their older brothers and sisters not to put their hands on a tram for fear of being electrocuted. When the new tram route was opened, the Mayor and Corporation officials could be seen on board amid gay decorations as it rattled on its way to the delight of spectators. Early in the morning women market traders brought flowers in season by tram from Devonport Market to sell in Plymouth.

The Athenaeum of The Plymouth Institution and The Theatre Royal, c 1868.
Duprez

The Theatre Royal provided varied entertainment of opera, "the popular Society play, the best class of melodrama and mirth compelling comedy", and was well attended at the time of the races and regatta. The students from The Royal Naval Engineering College frequently occupied the front seats of the stalls, and the female cast welcomed them backstage. The organ grinder was used to them persuading him to allow them to play his barrel organ. The theatre held 1192, and the top storey comprised a scene painting room and the stage machinery that could deal with the rapid changes of tableau required by the Victorian pantomime. the theatre was damaged by fire in 1863, and burnt out fifteen years later. Foulston used cast iron for much of the structural work of the interior; the proscenium arch had a span of sixty foot. The decorative gold scrollwork and the Regency stripe wall decor made this one of the most memorable provincial theatres west of London.

The Athenaeum Museum was revered for its collection of "four tattoed Maori heads of great rarity", porcelain, and The Barbican ducking chair. In the vestibule stood a plaster caste of The Medici Venus, the first classical nude seen in Plymouth; the original left Byron "dazzled and drunk with beauty". Erudite gentlemen passing the statue on their way to consult the scientific collection might have agreed with Byron, but they were used to the smell of the decaying collection of stuffed birds which was certainly no aphrodisiac.

The chaste Doric of The Athenaeum highlighted by The Great Blizzard of 1891. Residents in Athenaeum Street nearby were woken one morning by the sound of the Dorset Regimental band from The Citadel at the head of a crowd of fishermen armed with shovels and pick axes on their way to clear the frozen leat. The Crescent Gardens (right), the one time burial ground of the prisoners of war were reputably haunted.

Theatre Royal Hustings, 1868.
"We were at the hustings the whole day long watching the hourly returns and cheering our favourites, (Sir Robert Collier was returned). The throwing of decayed vegetables, addled eggs and flour was frequently resorted to, and the big trawler boys on the show of hands being called for cleared a large space in front of the returning officer by charging up and down through the crowd with a party coloured card attached to the end of a carter's whip. Thus the party supporters were able to show the largest area of hands".
H. Vigurs Harris (*Western Independent Centenary Number* 19/2/1933).

Heath

The Royal Hotel, "the most centrally situated for ocean passengers, the premier hotel of the West of England telephone no. 33" had a regular clientele of commercial travellers. The Dispense Bar was renowned for its West End atmosphere, and a bookmaker regularly kept a case of champagne for the use of his clients. The lodge to The Crescent Garden indicates the present day site of Westward Television. Only six of the fifteen houses originally projected by Dr. James Yonge, the owner of no. 15 (that had a coach house for five horses and probably the largest personal wine cellar in the Borough) had been built, and St. Andrew's vicarage stood in isolation on the corner of Athenaeum Street. There was a clear space between the cab rank and the theatre portico for H.M. Mail to arrive at full speed, set down its fare, turn round, and tear along Union Street at a terrific pace to Devonport.

The Royal Hotel "courtesy coach" collected passengers and luggage from the railway stations. Samuel Pearse the proprietor also supplied "superior carriages for weddings, posting and excursions; funerals were also arranged". The noise from the stableyard could be heard through the entrance arch in Athenaeum Place. There were 23 stalls 14 loose boxes, 2 large harness rooms and 3 large "motor" or coach houses for 20 carriages and waggonettes. At "The Hotel Shades" nearby was a long bar and smoking room. Here, one night a woman was turned upside down and filled up with best bitter.

In 1862, the year that Derry's Clock was erected, the trees that formerly screened the gloomy house of Dr. George Magrath, the distinguished but eccentric physician, at 8 George Terrace, were felled. The management of Harvey's Hotel effectively exorcised the ghost of that worthy by providing a bar where" gentlemen could enjoy their hookahs in the comfort of elbow chairs as pleasant as those in the first class carriages of The Great Western Railway".

George Street from Millbay Road, c 1868.
Duprez

The Palm Court, Royal Hotel
Green and gold Japanese leatherwork was used in the sumptuous £30,000 modernisation of The Royal Hotel in 1902. "The ante-drawingroom" was entered through a door that had drapings of mandarin silk. The Palm Court, famous for its orchestra and afternoon tea was decorated in white and gold; the palms were specially imported from Las Palmas. Attached to the hotel were The Assembly Rooms, where Plymouth Society came to play cards and dine. On Saturday nights, dances were held in Foulston's magnificent seventy-six feet long Regency ballroom. In 1882 the famous painting "Grace Darling" was exhibited here in "Mr. Wilson's great collection of nearly one thousand paintings."

William Derry, general carrier of 192 Union Street, agent to the Great Western and Cornwall Railways during his mayoralty (1862) gave only the "public clock" to Plymouth. The Corporation had to pay £300 for the architect-designed clock tower and took six months to find a suitable site. The decorative gilded ironwork was neglected and the drinking fountains remained dry much to the displeasure of the donor. This photograph clearly shows that the "four-faced deceiver" a name given to the clock by courting couples, justified their derision.

The tram for West Hoe and The Pier; the route was electrified in 1907.

The B.B.C. studio in Athenaeum Lane was conveniently situated for the famous Genoni's where those making their first broadcast could have a fortifying sherry. In 1882 Cousin's Hotel Buffet was redecorated "in delicate salmon tints" and the man about town could support "the elegantly marbled bar counter".

Rugg Monk

In front of the wine merchant's shop, a billboard man trundles his "perambulating machine" towards Baskerville's horsebus which is standing outside The Wiltshire and Dorset Bank. The late afternoon shadows are falling and the lamplighter is at work.

GEORGE STREET

George Street didn't change much prior to World War II. Now it is replaced by a carpark and the trees of Royal Parade at its intersection with Armada Way. A woman stands by her fishcart in front of the town offices of The Great Western Railway Company. Next door, Limpenny's umbrella shop also had a stock of officers' swagger canes and walking sticks. At The Domestic Bazaar any article cost 6½d. Nearby, the first taxi cab in Plymouth was on call for The Western Morning News offices to deliver papers to its agents. *"The Naval & Military Record"*, the only Service newspaper with correspondents in all Royal dockyards naval and military centres and all foreign stations was published here. "You have the ear of the lower deck as well as of the Officers' messes, more than anyone I know, perhaps not even Miss Weston", wrote Vice-Admiral Fitz-Gerald to the Editor.

George Street looking towards Bedford Street and The Globe Hotel, c 1868. Duprez
Next door to Joseph May Grose's hosier and glover's shop can be seen a small display of Michael Day's photographs. George Street shops were fashionable, and the ladies of Baxter & Simpson's millinery workroom made beaded frilled capes and satin garments. The principals visited Paris each season and returned with samples. They were patronised by the Queen of Roumania and Mrs. Cory of Langdon Court had a new outfit when Edward VII stayed at Wembury for the shoot. In 1895, The American Artificial Teeth Company offered country patients the service of a fitting in one afternoon after inspecting testimonials and specimens . . .

George Street Baptist Chapel, c 1868.

The site is now occupied by the Civic Centre. A Sunday School was held in the nearby *"Lyceum"*, where children of soldiers and sailors were taught during the week.

The Wiltshire and Dorset Bank.

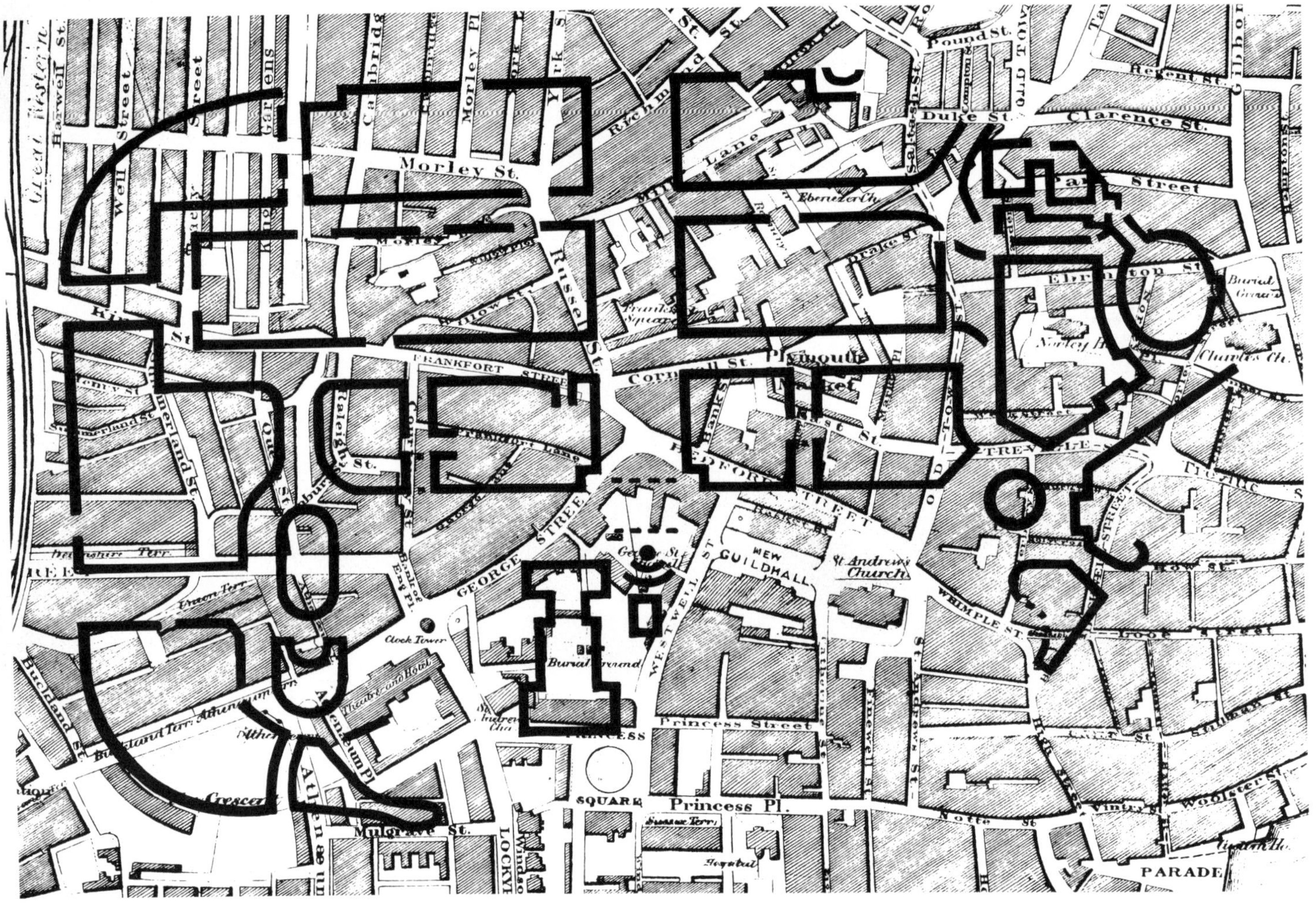

Bedford, Cornwall, and Frankfort Streets, c 1880. The post war town centre grid is superimposed.

Shopkeepers, fearing for their windows when 'Fogey' threw stones at boys he believed came from Stoke yelling "I knaws 'ee, you . . . 'Toke boys", gave him a few coppers to go away.

George Street where pavement chats had the background smell of freshly-ground aromatic coffee and the strains of musicians playing in Goodbody's cafe. Crab sandwiches at the Long Bar of *The Bodega* were popular. No females were allowed in The "Sawdust" Club there. Baskerville's bus can be seen on its way to Derry's Clock. The cry of an old man selling oysters could often be heard.

A canvas replica of Frankfort Gate made for The Royal Agricultural Show in 1890. Old bearded gentlemen stood on guard dressed as beefeaters, and were armed with pikes; the Globe Hotel can be seen on the left.

Bedford Street, c 1892
Watts' Globe was a family hotel and also catered for commercial travellers who could use its well appointed stockrooms. F. J. Kerswill next door in Frankfort Street assured the public that the leather for his hand-made shoes was curried and dressed by workmen of the town; thus enabling him "to extend local employment and have every branch under his immediate supervision". In Bank Street (right), women sold trays of violets and pansies; the dandies patronising The Plymouth Coffee House liked their long stemmed button holes on primrose day.

The Co-op building and hall by H. J. Snell on the corner of Courtenay Street (right); the clocktower in Frankfort Street was a well known landmark. Heath

Before this clock struck ten on Sunday morning women who had little time for shopping during the week and needed underwear to replace that damaged or lost in Union Street on the Saturday night were able to buy lingerie in a shop nearby in King Street. The penny seats at Linsdell's Star Hall of Varieties (known as 'The Penny Gaff'), were regularly taken by Royal Marine drummers and their girlfriends. The booing of the villain could be heard as one entered Frankfort Street. The scenery was painted in St. James Hall. Lindsell's also showed films and the ghost stories were popular. But when the permanent cinemas came to Plymouth, the premises reverted to being a shop once more.

"Don't squeeze me till I'm yours". Stanley Jay

Stallholders were out in all weathers till after ten o'clock at night, when the remaining stock on the barrow was sold at "the count-down". At Christmas, oranges, grapefruit and boxed dates topped the canvas awning. There was a skill carrying the maximum amount on the iron barrow from the store and obtaining a good pitch in Frankfort Street. By 7 a.m. Mrs. Burt pictured here had already made her customary trip to Devonport Market by tram and returned with cut flowers. Discomforts such as boils under the arms and the necessity to mangle rain-soaked corsets were made up for by a hot bath.

Harold Watson stallholder (right) and Frank Sparks in Frankfort Street c 1925.
Barrows were normally turned inwards, and moved at intervals as directed. "Striping" the barrows was a skill for which the Co-op used to charge £32 for their services.

Market Avenue looking towards Cornwall Street, 1896.
Beyond the shutters of the new Provision Market (right) can be seen Foulston's Regency Freemason's Hall on the corner of East Street. The Plymouth & Cottonian Library, also by him in Cornwall Street was blitzed. At the Meat Market in the 1920's rice and blood puddings sold for two a penny, or seven for threepence; a basket full of beef and bacon pieces cost one shilling and sixpence respectively. Outside, the old bootlace man stood in the road and cried "half a dozen laces for a penny, and a penny for six". "Market Gates" survived the war and were demolished when New George Street was constructed.

The Provision Market 1923. Martins of Plymstock's stall.

R. Scoble's 'Christmas Show, 1902.
Dennifords gold medal (at Sydney, Adelaide & London 1895) table and soda water manufactured nearby probably paired up on the same dinner table.

Tools for all trades. Lawson's old shop displaying as many tools as possible: adzes, chisels, hammers, handsaws, and grindstones. The premises have been rebuilt on the same site in Frankfort (now New George) Street.

The Drake Street entrance of The Provision. Market, 1923.
The Fat Stock Show was held here before the butchers dressed their shops for Christmas. In the Market, pigsheads with mouths kept wide open with apples or oranges, bladders of lard as big as footballs, and sticks of tripe could be seen. Mabel Martin, her son Alfred (left), Mr. Fred Uren purveyor of fruit and veg., Ernie Martin and Cicie, an assistant, are accompanied by a country stall holder. As a baby, Alfred slept under the stall. Nearby, were the hooplah stalls.

Frankfort Street in the 'Thirties.
The Western Morning News offices were rebuilt prior to the blitz and now are the only landmark left between Frankfort Street and the new Western Approach. King Street Methodist Chapel was on a site now occupied by shops in Frankfort Gate; this spacious pedestrian precinct, now that the trees are maturing has the feel of Rotterdam. The bronze statue of citizen Monsieur Jacques is a memory of that old city. It would be in the spirit of the former King Street life to have a statue of Pratt the organ grinder and his monkey Bruce for children to see who find it difficult to imagine the workaday Plymouth that their grandfathers recall.

The intersection of Frankfort, Bedford, Cornwall and Russell Streets, Christmas 1938.
The stallholders can be seen on the left hand side of Frankfort Street. Dick Burt's laden barrow is in the foreground. The bye-laws concerning street cries and traffic obstruction were vigorously enforced. Marquand's lorry is loaded with crates, and Stevens' three wheeler van is on its way to deliver pasties.

PROGRAMME.

BUGLER LAKE

KID KELLY

Great Fifteen Three-minute-Rounds Contest,

BUGLER LAKE

(Stonehouse), Ex-Bantam-weight Champion of England and Europe; *versus*

KID KELLY

(C.B.C.), Plymouth.

Extra Special 10-Rounds Bantam-weight Return Contest,

PERCY LAKE v. YOUNG JINKS
Devonport. S.B.C.

8-Rounds Welter-weight Contest,

D. BURT v SEAMAN DIXON
S.B.C. H.M.S. Frobisher.

8-Rounds Feather-weight Contest, **J. Simpson v. Sea. Allman** C.B.C. H.M.S Thunderer.	8-Rounds Bantam-weight Contest, **Seaman Patton v A. Mills** R.N. Bks., I.S.B.A. C.A.C. Champ., 1924.
8-Rounds Fly-weight Contest, **J. Sheppard v. Sea. Doherty** C.B.C. R.N. Barracks.	4-Rounds Paper-wt. Contest, **P. [illegible]aw v. B. Swift's Nipper** C.B.C.
6-Rounds Fly-weight Contest, **Bob Lewis v. Tom French** Truro. C.B.C.	6-Rounds Feather-weight Contest, **A. Taylor v. A. Smith** Formerly of Plympton, now of Torquay. Plymouth.

By request, **JOE SYMONDS,** Ex. Fly wt. Champion and **BILLY SWIFT,** Ex. Bantam-wt. Champion of the West of England, will box 3 Exhibition Rounds.

MUSIC by the BAND under the Baton of MR. PERCY J. HAM.

The Sugar Refinery Mill Street, 1908, where twenty-eight pound sugar cones like dunces' caps were sold to merchants. Nearby at "The Winter Gardens" W. C. & S. Hancock's Grand Circus and Menagerie was for twopence *"the cheapest and most varied entertainment in 'The Three Towns'"*. In 1900 women impersonated men there; Romeos, acrobats, a lady in a trance and high-kicking artistes were also billed. Added incentives were baby shows and a challenge to drag a 280 lb. sack of flour round the ring, as well as the varied sideshows. At the 6.30 to 10.30 p.m. and afternoon performances at 3 p.m. on Wednesday and Saturday; Pratt the organ grinder "had an engagement to play his hurdy gurdy on the stage outside the lions cages, and several girls dressed in bright picturesque dresses and headgear danced the corkscrew dance" to his music.

A programme of the grand complementary benefit for the retiring boxing promotor Harry Jenkins on Friday, February 13th, 1925. Percy Ham was a professional band master; Bugler Lake, who later turned professional started his boxing career when in the Royal Marines. Kid Kelly of The Caprera Boxing Club was considered a "genuine little sport and a sure trier whoever his opponent might be". On Friday nights at The Cosmopolitan Gymnasium, the band played Dick Burt's signature tune "Yes, we have no bananas" before the match commenced. Jack Johnson fought at "The Cosmo", and Agnes Weston successfully petitioned The Plymouth Watch Committee that the film of the fight W. & E. Linsdell were intending to show there on Boxing Day 1910 should not be seen.

An aerial view of the site of Royal Parade. The Co-op Building can be seen on the left, and right, a turret of The Prudential Building.

Rugg Monk 1892

The back of the old Market looking towards East Street, where Spooner's 'house furnishers' and William Alsford's dining rooms can be seen. At Plimsaul Bros. Ironmongers, also in East Street "cooking ranges, brass bedsteads, tea urns and gas chandeliers in glass ormolu and artistic bronze" were sold.

The East Street corner of Market Alley, which in 1903 became The Bedford Arcade. At No. 6 and 7, were the premises of Henry Whitfeld, "The People's Brushmaker".

Izzett Knight's Tailor Shop and "the shunt off" for trams at Old Town Avenue 1896; a site now partly occupied by Boots' and Marks & Spencer's stores.
Market Place pubs, *The Golden Lion, Old Cattle Market* and *Chester Cup* (left) were well patronised by the country carriers and the crowds that gathered on Saturday nights to see the cheapjacks sell their wares by the light of naptha flares. Occasionally there were rough scenes when the barrows got tipped over. Tommy Gaskin, "The Chocolate Kid" enlivened the proceedings: "I'm not asking 5/-, nor 4/- not even 1/- but 3d.", and hastily sold his sweets. A cement seller cried out "I can stick anything but a broken heart". Phil Strong sold embrocation and demonstrated the strength that it was supposed to give with a set of chest expanders. Onlookers waited for him to pull number 6, the most enormous, but he never obliged. There were other entertainments including a juggler who made your money disappear, and the soapbox orators. Sequah the herbalist provided a public dental service: "if four gentlemen will step up into the carriage and hold the screen around, I will operate while the band plays." Shoppers found most requirements here from cheap rolls of canvas (the poorer man's fitted carpet) to hedgehog's grease for rheumatism.

The Butcher's stalls in the Old Market, 1892. Rugg Monk
Farmers' wives wearing long riding habits came here on horseback. A smallholder at Tamerton occasionally slaughtered a pig at 2.30 a.m., hung it, and sold it before proceeding to work at the Dockyard.

The Old Corn Exchange and Fish Market, c 1892. Rugg Monk
On Thursdays the farmers, millers and corn merchants braded. The millers always heard of an increase in corn prices by telegraph. News of a decline in price arrived by stage coach. At the Fishmarket, skins of sole were laid out to dry on the slabs of slate and sold to the brewery to clear the beer.

Infantry procession Old Town Street, 1896.
When the Tichbourne Claimant arrived at Mutley Station a crowd of supporters accompanied him down Old Town Street.
Behind The Bedford Vaults (right) market traders stabled their "pony and jingle" (2 or 3 people could sit either side and there was a door in the back) at The Caxton Mews.

Courtyard in Saltash Street, in the vicinity of Central Hall. Dove's Cottages have gone, and with them the "domestic industry" of the staymaker who lived in the first cottage.

The junction of Saltash Street and Old Town Street, c 1896. Fairweather's draper's shop is on the corner of Drake Street. Jaspers sold cardboard collars and cuffs, also shirtfronts ('paper dickies').

Saltash Street Corner, Old Town Street. Rugg Monk. Drake Circus underpass at the end of Cornwall Street now occupies this site. The old *Noah's Ark* was famed for its spicy brew of white ale. The impressive iron gates are the entrance to The Ebenezer Chapel now The Central Hall; the approach was at this time flanked by trees. Around the corner was the Excel Dairy and Mill Street where at Carter's saddlers shop horse brasses for harnesses could be bought. Walter's forage was handy for ostlers.

Cobourg Street
George Jago of Liskeard was headmaster of The Public School in Cobourg Street for forty-three years and retired in 1885. His son Mr. Charles and the two Miss Jagos ran the school on the Lancastrian system. When Isaac Foot attended this school fees were 7/6d. per quarter.
The organ grinder was often to be found here entertaining the children.

Crowds on the corner of Tavistock Place welcome home the South African detachment of The Second Prince of Wales Devon Volunteers from The Boer War in 1901. Rugg Monk

"Lord Roberts and Kitchener, General Buller and White, all went to South Africa to have a jolly good fight. Now the war is over, oh how happy I will be for I love sweet Rosy O'Grady; sweet Rosy O'Grady loves me"'

Tram Stop at the junction of Tavistock Place and Old Town Street, c 1895.
Rugg Monk
On the left, Clarence, Park and Ebrington Streets have been cleared for the construction of Charles Street and Drake Circus shopping precinct. *The Revenue Hotel* (right) and Duke Street that ran through to Saltash Street, were the last landmarks to disappear.

Tavistock Road Francis Frith

By 1891 the present reservoir had been constructed, and the columns from the Old Plymouth Market near the site of the present day St. Andrew's Cross roundabout were re-erected as a colonnade; nearby are the old cottages later removed. In the early morning, children would go to the bakers before school with their pillow-cases to get sixpence worth of stale bread and cake.

Sherwell House, c 1865.
The house and grounds have now been covered by Queen Anne Terrace.
There were complaints about the lack of trees near the City centre when a sycamore was felled to make snuff boxes for the Mayor and corporation officials. In 1907 C. E. Eldred, R.N. wrote in *Devonia* "there is probably no town whose environs have suffered like Plymouth from the ruthless advances of the jerrybuilder. Mansions and their grounds that once commanded superb prospects of The Sound are being rapidly covered by rows and rows of unsightly terraces repeated ad nauseam".

Mutley Plain, May 1896.
The horse trams to and from The Market and Compton Lane had canvas curtains. If it was raining, the journey would be made in semi darkness.

A smartly dressed foreman supervises the 'works' in Tavistock Road. The gateway to his left survives. The trees are in the grounds of Sherwell House.

Mutley Plain, June 1895.
The camels of Bostock's Circus, accompanied by "hundreds of living specimens and novelties never seen before in the provinces, "on their way to Millbay Drill Hall where "the steam organ connected to the whirligig, the menagerie band and the crack of rifles in the shooting galleries" thrilled the children. "An old brown bear danced a scottish reel all to himself accompanied by a man playing a cornet."

Barge's new delivery cart. Inside the shop at Mutley Plain was a "Public telephone".

Mutley Plain, May 1896
A bullock waggon advertises suet. Advertising to catch the attention of the shopper was carefully thought out: The manager of Liptons instructed that a pig should be driven through the city with "shop at Liptons" painted on its hide, whilst Spooner's mobile shops were drawn by mules.

Mutley Station

The interior of Barge's Belgrave Pharmacy, Mutley Plain, 1896. He also had another shop in Old Town Street.

A horse tram passing Mutley Grammar School, 1896.
Women who used the upper deck sometimes were not aware that the conductor could see their ankles or perhaps their knees as they climbed the open metal stairs.

Old Town Street looking towards Treville Street Corner and *The Rose & Crown* Francis Frith
In the foreground is Balkwill's pharmaceutical chemist (formerly Cookworthy) established in 1725; The hire department could provide water beds, pillows, cushions, crutches, armslings, bedrests, carryin g and wheelchairs.

SPOONER'S CORNER

Sun Buildings and "new" Spooner's Corner.

A horse tram follows two electric trams up Bedford Street towards Spooner's Corner. The track in the foreground leads to Basket Street, the narrowest part of the route. The railings on the right surround St. Andrew's Cross; the gate piers are the only survivors in what is now Royal Parade.

Looking up Old Town Street, to East Street and Treville Street intersection. Opposite Chubb's Hotel at 95/96 Old Town Street, Densham's Dandelion Pills were prepared from the "milky juice of the root, and aided digestion". New shops replaced the *Old Four Castles* and *The Rose & Crown*, and housed a cinema built to resemble a large saloon railway coach with "an American Observation car".

One of the most spectacular fires witnessed in Plymouth was at Spooner's drapery store in 1902. The crowds have gathered to see the return of the soldiers from South Africa in 1901. Little boys had learnt to sing this sone accompanied by a barrel organ, proudly sticking out their chests and clenching their fists manfully.

"The Boers have got my Daddy,
my soldier Dad,
I don't like to hear my Mammy
sigh, I don't like to see my
Mammy cry. I'm going in a big
ship across the raging sea,
I'm going to fight the Boers
and bring my Daddy back to me."

Old Town Street decorated for Queen Victoria's Jubilee, 1897.

The photographer probably stood in the vicinity of the public telephone boxes near the foot of the Eastlake Walk escalator.
The old gables gave the street its winding character, but this was largely removed by Victorian redevelopment.

The Rose & Crown, Old Town Street seen from the corner of Week Street, c 1895.   Rugg Monk

An old house demolished to make way for Old Town Avenue; many of the houses in Old Town Street were formerly thatched. In 1841, a woman who kept a tripe shop in the street could remember Dr. Johnson walking past her door.

"Works in progress" obstruct an electric tram where now informal landscaping and benches occupy the area between old Ebrington Street corner and New George Street which now cuts a swathe through the old meat market; Market Avenue and the top of old Cornwall Street can be seen in the middle distance.

The tramway depot, Ebrington Street. Rugg Monk

Old Ebrington Street Corner, now part of the perimeter of Drake Circus shopping precinct, (Eastlake Street). Rugg Monk

F. C. Heard,,
"Plymouth Celebrity"
Prior's Stoke news agency'

Street hawkers could be seen in Old Town Street. One man sold Old Moore's Almanac and railway time-tables. The muffin man was often seen at street corners.

Drake Circus, c 1903, Garden Street was redeveloped later. Dustmen were equipped with long handled shovels to shovel refuse into the horse-drawn cart.

When The Corporation proposed to run electric trams through Old Town Street, traders raised great opposition because they argued that ladies would not stop their carriages there because of the trams; consequently part of the street was set back and it was decided to call this "improvement" Drake Circus, an idea that had found favour after the tercentenary celebrations of The Armada.

Rugg Monk

"A horse tram leaving Market Terminus."
Old Town Avenue, c 1896.
At this point where Ebrington Street joined Old Town Street it was little wider than a lane. Ebrington House Tailors has already been demolished; in their turn followed Mountstephen's Cutlers, Medlen's jewellers, and Underhill's premises.

The Old Four Castles, Old Town Street, c 1895.
Rugg Monk
This old tavern sold wine, spirits, porter and tobacco. The good stabling it advertises was on the site of Burton the tailors.
Many shopkeepers lived over their premises some of which were old established businesses. In 1884, Colliers the wine merchants had a new decor of "green velvet curtains, sateen blinds in the windows, turkish carpets on the floor and comfortable chairs" that were favourably commented on in "*The Western Figaro*"; totally different, they claimed, "from the conventional gauze blinds, canvas floor covering, mahogany counter and hard stools."

Wesley Chapel, Ham Street, 1877. John Hawke
The building was designed by a local architect, H. J. Snell, and subsequently became Selleck's Wesley restaurant after it was burnt. Prior to this the road outside was lined with carriages on Sundays. Nearby, a blind man accompanied his wife on the accordian and the cinema queues, some of whom had paid their "halfpenny worth of electicity" to come here by tram, enjoyed their songs.

Lanyon's seventeenth century Almshouses, Green Street, with accommodation for forty-two poor people adjacent to Charles Church. This photograph was taken prior to the rebuilding in 1868. Notice the moorland granite columns.

Small lock-up shops in Ebrington Street on the site of the northern sub-way at Charles Church roundabout. At Norley House (left) behind Old Town Street, the home of the Arthur family, brewers, lived George Arthur who later was Knighted for his services as colonial administrator, governor of Van Dieman's Land, Upper Canada and Bombay.

Ebrington Street looking towards Old Town Street, c 1893.

Charles Church seen from Vennel Street, c 1880.
Formerly there were stately elms in this large churchyard where William Derry and other leading citizens were buried. In Green Street, the Soup Kitchen sold penny plates of soup or rice, and in the evenings, Mr. Kelly the chimney-sweep sold ½d. meat pies from an oven on his cart. Sometimes horses coming up the slope in Green Street would shie when they saw their reflections in the shop windows. Charles Boys School had a fife and drum parade; in 1914, a Navy whaler was used for their geography and nature studies. Before the Victorians restored Charles Church, the pews were so high that the congregation complained of stiff necks if they looked up steadfastly at the preacher.

Charles Church Vicarage, Norley Street, (demolished 1944), where Robert Stephen Hawker (1804-1875), later vicar of Morwenstow, stayed with his evangelist grandfather, a popular preacher who founded the first Sunday School in Plymouth, "The Household of Faith" in Vennel Street.

Hawker of Charles Church. He was curate, then vicar 1784-1827. This early photograph of a silhouette was found in a volume of his sermons.

On Monday mornings the Rev. Septimus Courtenay, Vicar of Charles Church (1832-1843) gave his "lectures" in the dark in winter.

"The Old Nappertacle", Bretonside, c 1896. Rugg Monk Plymouth women, incredulous that the Cornish fishermen could sing so well, used to come into the alley to hear them on Sundays. The Old Tabernacle was bought by the North Quay Working Men's Mission in 1888.

The palatial premises of the Naval Bank on the corner of Kinterbury and Whimple Streets.

Kinterbury Street.
Many of these houses were used as warehouses and rag stores; some were jettied. One Queen Anne house had slate carvings of playing cards.
Formerly the street ran from Whimple Street to Treville Street, but has been rerouted and shortened.

Waggonette Outing
Buckwell Street, 1898.
W. Green, beer retailer at *The Crown & Septre*, welcomed the Barbican fishermen. The waggonette was stabled in High Street, and this was no doubt the first stopping place for Allsopp's Pale Ales. The outing is men only, and the curtains are twitching, but the fish hawker standing with her basket outside Jones' fish merchants will tell all.

Stillman Street, "where pigs and fowls were bred in cellars and gardens without check or remonstrance."
John Hine, architect of the Victorian Guildhall, had this photograph taken of the birthplace of John Kitto, the biblical scholar and eastern traveller, in 1860.

Outside Pitts' Grain Stores and *The Salutation Inn,* Stillman Street, 1892. Rugg Monk
"One of the rare places in the West Country where barley is prepared for the brewers. The golden grain is spread on the long clean floor." Micky Antonucci made his famous icecream that he served with pink corn oil in Batter Street. Before morning lessons he was assisted by schoolboys.

"Lovely 'arbour mackerell two a penny." (Looe Street pubs were known for their crustacean smell.) "The ground rises abruptly, and slippery half-worn limestone steps lead to houses more ruinous and more crowded than those fronting the street." (Rawlinson, 1853).
Here at the top of the hill once lived Sir Francis Drake before he purchased Buckland Abbey.

Looe Street, c 1896. R. Monk

Punch & Judy Show in Vauxhall Court, 1896.
A woman stood at the entrance to the court and collected the money. The show could also be seen at The Parade and on The Barbican Quay.

"Johno from St. Malo"
Rugg Monk
"Say what will you geeve." For sixpence and "a couple of pennies for myself" the longest string was handed over. Their wives skinned and threaded the onions by their beds in a warehouse at North Quay. Farley's shop in Exeter Street baked long loaves for them.

36 Looe Street, the first house to be restored by The Barbican Association Ltd. William Dear, Bottle Merchant, lived here. He gave ½d. for a two pound jam jar. For that money, children could buy six or seven bruised apples.

Looe Street, c 1880.
"Clogs as light as a dancing shoe." The onion seller later used a bicycle.

Whimple Street, c 1868. Duprez
The Old Post Office (right) housed the first pioneer telephone exchange in Devon and Cornwall in 1881. The Bayly family of Torr House, Plymouth, friends of Eddison Bell were the first to have a private telephone.
The Naval Bank, the pawnshop, and, sadly, Pickens' sawdust Bar, in whose snug women could enjoy a jug of ale, have now gone along with the Old Guildhall with its illuminated clock. The tower was flanked by police offices and cells.

Buckwell Street, c 1890. Rugg Monk
Where J. H. Stephens, surgeon and mechanical dentist sold Parrott's celebrated anti cholera mixture. Patients were waited upon at their residences if required. All the houses on the left hand side of the street have been replaced, and the entrance to How Street widened. Holycross Lane leading to Kinterbury Street has been eliminated by the new approach to the Bus Station.

Slate hung houses in Bretonside, c 1898. Rugg Monk
The shops left to right facing Vauxhall Street are M. Antonucci, dealer in ice cream, Mrs. Mitchelmore draper, and H. Tall lamp dealer. On the corner of Green Street is Pengelly's saddler's shop.

Horse bus in Bedford Street, c 1868. St. Andrew's Churchyard can be seen on the left, and old Basket Street.
Duprez

Bedford Street, c 1868. Duprez
Horse tram drivers kept free of chest trouble when they wore a brown paper vest rubbed with goose oil next to the skin. Some purchased 2d. worth of straw to put in their boots to prevent chilblains.

St. Andrew's Cross was unveiled on May 30th, 1895. The Post Office is at the end of Guildhall Square, and Basket Street.

Basket Street, c 1868, looking towards Westwell Street (now Armada Way).
It is difficult to imagine "young women skinning the withes" to make lobster pots, a fowl run and kitchen garden opposite John Yeo's store in Royal Parade today.

"The Old Church Twelves Almshouses" St. Andrew's Church Alley, c 1865. This range of buildings and those as far as The Synagogue in Catherine Street were demolished, c 1870. Note the advertisements including one for Latchley Devon Great Consuls, and the mobile fire escape.

Banjomen in Bedford Street, c 1892. Rugg Monk
These men are publicising a circus. The buskers wore white trousers and straw hats and entertained the theatre queues.

St. Andrew's Church, c 1869, before the Victorian restoration. The building (left) popularly known as "The Prysten House" was owned by John Yogge who gave money for the massive church tower to be built. In 1884 Messrs. Brown Wills & Nicholson used the premises for stores, and "the Abbey" was well-known for its hams pickled here in the gloom. Salt fish, tapioca, bags of barcelonas, boxes of oranges and sugar loaves were warehoused on the upper floors. Some rooms grew mould and mildew and were only fit for storing jars of vitriol. After the final restoration by A. S. Parker in 1928, a beer mug which had been found in the old wine cellar was filled with ginger flavoured ale and given to "The Prior of Plympton" in the historical pageant at the re-opening on the 29th November.

The interior of St. Andrew's Church was rearranged by John Foulston in 1828. Most of the pews were rented but thirty-six of them were occupied by officials of the Corporation who didn't pay a farthing for the privilege. Dr. Johnson visited his friend the vicar, Zachariah Mudge and sprawled in one of the box pews and listened to the sermons. The head of the old vicar wearing a scarlet nightcap was momentarily seen by Frederick Bone the churchwarden when his vault to the right of the altar was opened.

The Hospital of Poor's Portion, Catherine Street, c 1869. Prior to the building being occupied by the town authorities, "Divers Godly persons of the counties of Devon Dorset and Somerset" met here in March 1630 before they set sail to found The Dorchester Church Colony, the oldest part of Boston. The ministers John Maverick and John Warham chiselled their motto over the door "By God's helpe through Christ". When this photograph was taken, the building was no longer in use as a workhouse, and a bookbinder had premises here.

The nave of St. Andrew's Church, c 1870. The Marine band in gorgeous attire with horsetail plumes in their hats played their way into church on Sundays.

John Bargus Yonge photographed in Plymouth 1861 wearing the 'rifle uniform' of the Second Devon Rifle Volunteers who formed in 1859. They drilled in the courtyard of the Grammar School (orphans aid charity) at Catherine Street (right).

The old Workhouse, c 1869.

3 p.m., Thursday, 28th July, 1870.
W. Luscombe, Mayor, Dr. Wilkinson, vicar of St. Andrew's, the architects, Messrs. A. Norman and J. Hine (middle), the contractors Messrs. Call & Pethick (far left) and mace bearers. During the time exposure the workman on the left moved his trowel. In 1874 at the Theatre Royal John Riley Newcombe the lessee put on a pantomime where figures resembling the Mayor and Town Clerk in their robes of office and the chief of Police danced a sarabande followed by a "cherokee war gallop" cheered by a packed house. The corporation however threatened legal action because of this redicule. In reply to their letter of censure and reprobation Newcombe in spite of the risk of losing his lease commented "like myself, you are the servants of the public and must expect your deeds to be criticised. I am your servant, but not your menial."

Borough of Plymouth.

NEW GUILDHALL.

LAYING FOUNDATION STONE.

The Right Worshipful The MAYOR will lay the Foundation Stone of the New Buildings On THURSDAY next (the 28th instant), at Three p m.

The Mayor will meet the Magistrates, Council, &c., at the GUILDHALL, at 2.30 p.m., and walk thence in Procession to the spot.

Order of Procession.

POLICE.
CONTRACTORS.
ARCHITECTS' CLERKS, BEARING IMPLEMENTS.
ARCHITECTS,
TOWN SURVEYOR.
CORPORATE OFFICERS.
COUNCILLORS.
ALDERMEN.
MAGISTRATES.
TOWN SERGEANTS, BEARING MACES.
VICAR OF ST. ANDREWS. THE MAYOR. TOWN CLERK.
POLICE.

(POLICE. on either side)

On arriving at the Site the Vicar of St. Andrews will offer up Prayer.

The Chairman of the Committee (Mr. ROOKER) will then address the Mayor, and request him to lay the Stone.

On the Mayor's replying, acceding to the request, he will be presented by the Architects with a Silver Trowel, and under their instructions declare the "FOUNDATION STONE" well and truly laid.

Admission to the Platform by Tickets only. The Area will be open to the Public.

After the Ceremony the Mayor and Corporation will return to the Guildhall, and there will be (at 5 p.m.) a Public Commemorative Dinner at the Royal Hotel.

By Order,

C. W. CROFT, *Chamberlain.*

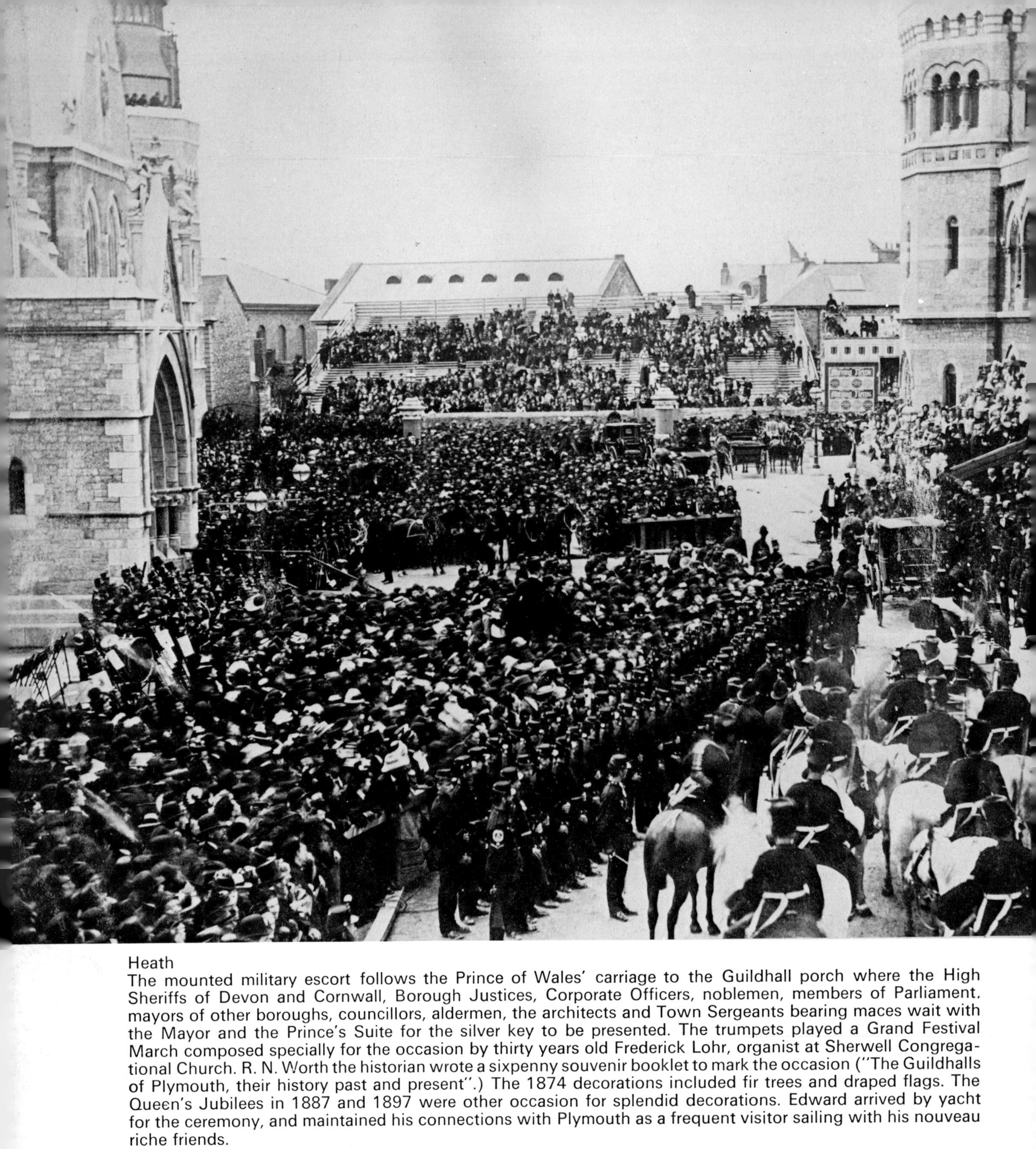

Heath
The mounted military escort follows the Prince of Wales' carriage to the Guildhall porch where the High Sheriffs of Devon and Cornwall, Borough Justices, Corporate Officers, noblemen, members of Parliament, mayors of other boroughs, councillors, aldermen, the architects and Town Sergeants bearing maces wait with the Mayor and the Prince's Suite for the silver key to be presented. The trumpets played a Grand Festival March composed specially for the occasion by thirty years old Frederick Lohr, organist at Sherwell Congregational Church. R. N. Worth the historian wrote a sixpenny souvenir booklet to mark the occasion ("The Guildhalls of Plymouth, their history past and present".) The 1874 decorations included fir trees and draped flags. The Queen's Jubilees in 1887 and 1897 were other occasion for splendid decorations. Edward arrived by yacht for the ceremony, and maintained his connections with Plymouth as a frequent visitor sailing with his nouveau riche friends.

The ceremony at The Door of Unity, and the dedication of the memorial to the American officers, 30th May, 1930. Those present included the American Ambassador, members of The Daughters of 1812 and the Bishop of Exeter. Lady Nancy Astor, accompanied by her husband, exchanges a witty aside with Dr. Harry Moreton the organist.

1897 Jubilee arch in Guildhall Square, (note the thirty foot ladder.) Children celebrated the occasion too (right).

Scientific Exhibition, St. Andrew's Hall, c 1876, (built on the old St. Andrew's vicarage garden, later the post office and now an ornamental pond outside the Civic Centre).

"The Mayor holding a Pike", Burrator, 1901. Rugg Monk
Joseph Arthur Bellamy, Spanish Vice Consul and Manager of Luscombe & Bellamy, Consuls and ship agents, was responsible for sanitation.

The statue to the Liberal Alfred Rooker in Guildhall Square. Tory Party members saw that the former orator was placed as near as possible to the public toilets. Life size statues were placed on top of the Guildhall. Each gable had one including those of Edward I, Hawkins, Frobisher, and others. The six panels each side of the porch represent Painting, Sculpture, Astronomy, Mechanics, Architecture, Music, Commerce, Plenty, Law, Peace, War, and Religion.

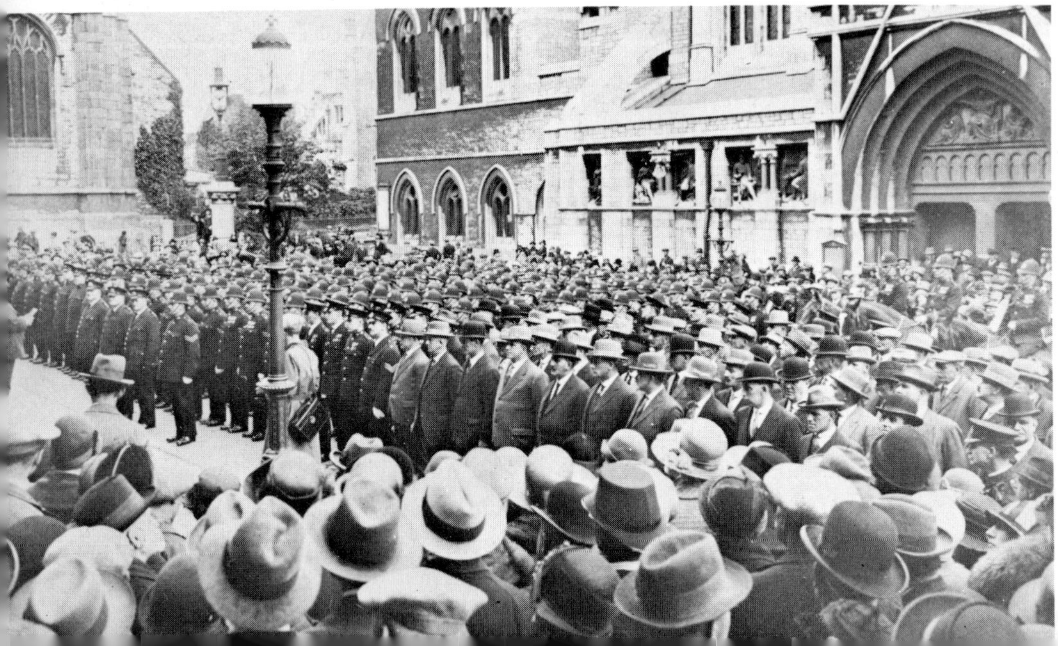

Guildhall Square, 1926
The special constables being briefed at the time of the General Strike, 1926. George Ebury the local Communist Party leader told his supporters to behave themselves for "if the Military are called in brothers, God help you."

Ye Fyshinge Feaste, c 1870.
"The claret and lemon was consumed long before dinner was served at 4 p.m. When we arrived the trout were frizzling in the pan." (Editor *Western Figaro* 29/8/1884). The ceremonial goblet filled with pure water from the weirhead can be seen as the Mayor is about to propose the toast "to the pious memory of Sir Francis Drake".

"The massive grandeur" of the interior of The Great Hall that seated 2,600. The tables are laid for the dinner to celebrate the opening of The Guildhall. The first night life in Plymouth was provided by "The Cafe Chantant" at The Guildhall. The Saturday concerts were popular, and a number of massive oratorios were performed: Gounod's "The Redemption", Sullivan's "Golden Legends" and Elgar's "Dream of Gerontius". "For those that come with credentials to local society there are the assembly balls. Brilliant Naval and Military dances occur with tolerable frequency during Winter and Spring." On August 21st, 1877 Eddison Bell demonstrated his telephone by playing on a telephone organ resembling a harmonium "God Save the Queen" which was clearly heard in The Guildhall.

A carriage approaching Spooners Corner, 1896.
In the foreground are "the six pendant lamps" installed when the shopfront was renewed in 1889. The gentry were seen in Bedford Street during the morning. Middle class ladies preferred to take afternoon tea and listen to the cafe orchestras.

Bedford Street, 1895.
Rugg Monk
A travelling circus has left Millbay Drill Hall and takes the opportunity to get the maximum publicity. Fortunately the procession with its entourage didn't have to go under the Union Street arch.

"Don't feed the elephants".
When the circus went to Cornwall, the elephants towed the vehicles to the Torpoint Ferry.

Rugg Monk 1895

Bedford Street Hatter, 1865.

Bedford Street, 1901. Rugg Monk

Bedford Street, 1902.
The Stoke horse bus en route from St. Andrew's Church via Millbridge toll gate, passes *The Borough Arms* in Bank Street corner opened by The Plymouth Coffee House Company in October 1878. In the downstairs bar were newspaper stands where the London and local papers could be consulted. There were handsome marble tables and comfortable chairs on all floors. W. D. Howells, a visiting American wrote in 1905, "I saw a great prosperity around me, and no sign of the hustle that is supposed to create it with us."

Travelling circus at Perkin Brothers' Corner, Bedford Street, 1898. Rugg Monk

A story is told that "Peggy" Hancock used to poke the lion's ribs with his wooden leg through the cage bars. On one never to be forgotten occasion the door opened and the lion fell out. The alarm was raised and the doors of the meat market nearby were closed. On investigation, however, it was found that the lion had false teeth.

The Prudential Building on the site of the old Globe Hotel was a landmark that survived the blitz. Downstairs in the smoking lounge of The Globe Restaurant & Grill, the appointments page of *The Evening Herald* was avidly read and commented upon by officers who sometimes first learnt about their new appointments there, when they took afternoon tea at a cost of sixpence. On rugger nights, they danced with local debutantes, and the merrymaking of the younger men could be heard through the marble veined walls of the toilets.

Carriages from the meeting of The Royal Agricultural Society's Exhibition reception at The Guildhall on their way down Bedford Street, 1898. Rugg Monk

Bedford Street was renowned for its old established shops. In November 1884 Popham's toyroom was hung with Chinese lanterns made to represent birds, beasts and fishes, for "The Fancy Fair". Amongst the 2,000 dolls in stock there were the familiar English favourites "with impossibly blue eyes and golden hair, crying dolls and those that say ma-ma at the slightest provocation". There were also little almond-eyed dolls with pursed up lips and hideous ears from China and Japan. Yeo's was famous for its blankets. Men from the Royal Marine band played at Goodbody's restaurant in the afternoons, and George East's orchestra could be heard at Dingles.
In the window of Bearus' jewellers shop in the Bedford Arcade were two live bear cubs. A sandwich board man advertised the firm's merchandise. He was seven feet tall and used to light his cigarette from a street lamp.

Guildhall Square, 1874, before Westwell Street was widened.
The Guildhall, Law Courts and Municipal Offices cost £50,000. Rev. S. Baring Gould wrote in his Devon Little Guide that "it might have been better and it might have been worse". Alfred Waterhouse whose Manchester Town Hall received acclaim, selected the winning design from the competition. The Guildhall Square was a focal point and dances were held here on New Year's Eve. On the stroke of twelve, the Mayor appeared on the balcony of the Municipal Building to wish the crowd good tidings for the new year. After that people quietly dispersed, but there had been an air of conviviality, the feeling that most of the towns-people had been present within the confines of the Square.

The Y.M.C.A. moved into their new premises on the corner of Westwell Street and Bedford Street in 1887. The photograph (on the left) shows the site before redevelopment.
Rugg Monk

Blundell's dray in Westwell Street. Behind the tram is the Post Office. The Guildhall tower is on the right. C. Frank

Mr. Alfred Churchill, his son Randolph, and the staff of The Fisheries. Locally caught sturgeon were sent by them to the Royal table.
The Cookworthy family vault was in the old burial ground behind the shop. The trees survive as part of the Civic Centre garden.

Allen's chemist shop at The Island House, Westwell Street (now the site of the underpass at Royal Parade), and the premises of The Devon & Cornwall Banking Company Bedford Street (later Lloyds). The Manager kept a small farm near Plymouth. Every week a cow was brought into the garden at the back of the bank so that the children could be provided with fresh milk.

Princess Square, c 1868. Duprez
The gardens in the square were ultimately neglected and all kinds of refuse was pitched in and left there, apparently without rebuke. This was considered to be a suitable site for the first car park in Plymouth. Princess Square now forms part of Armada Way.

Entertainments at The Mechanic's Institute (middle left) in 1865 (when The Royal Agricultural Society of England held their show at Plymouth) included "delineations of Negro life" from Templeton's Minstrels "the only original African Opera troupe" every evening at 8 p.m. Tom Thumb later appeared there, and his carriage was drawn around the street by "the most diminutive ponies in show business". The crenellated stone Camera Obscura on The Hoe was afterwards known as "Tom Thumb's Castle".
In 1900, scholars had 2d. privilege tickets to see "The exhibition of animated photographs" being shown at the Mechanic's Institute.

Hoegate Dr. Leach "The Modern Naturalist" was born in the room over the arch. The last owner, T. W. Fox claimed that undesirable people hid in the street, and despite protests the gatehouse was demolished in 1863.

The South Devon & East Cornwall Hospital, Sussex Terrace (now Notte Street), c 1868. Duprez
The Earl of Mount Edgcumbe gave money for a ward to be fitted up for the reception of additional patients, on the payment of ten shillings a week which was the actual cost of maintenance in 1865. On Wednesday, 26th August, 1868, Mr. Browne of The Plymouth Town Mission held a service in each ward: "I found the inmates in a good state of mind for hearing the word, and very thankful". In 1884 a new hospital was built at Greenbank.

Tucker, the Town Crier at Plymouth Market, 1837. J. C. Harris

The Turk's Head Inn, St. Andrew's Street, c 1860.
The aleconner when testing beer wore leather shorts. One method was to spill some "accidentally" on the wooden settle and sit down on it. If his bottom adhered to the seat, the landlord had been caught out. John Hine, architect of The Guildhall thought that the narrow streets in the old town should not be widened, and the picturesque gables replaced by "gaunt shopfronts enlivened by merely a couple of 18 penny urns" (1861).

Old houses in St. Andrew's Street.
Number 33 survives and was formerly a licensed refreshment house. The iceworks, the opposite side of the street, produced twenty tons of ice daily in 1900.
Number 12 Notte Street (later the Artizans' dwellings, demolished 1963) "where a few rampant lions struggle to make their way through the narrow cages that do duty as brackets. There are the occasional representations of chubby boys indifferently clad, but disporting with flowers of marvellous growth."

Bull Hill (now Buckwell Street), c 1920.
Where fashion conscious Plymouth women tried Mr. Matthews' very own "ivy cling" shingle. Schoolboys had to aclimatise after one of his famous "all offs."

Houses in High Street, c 1879, that in 1853 "gave shelter to the improvident, the viscious and the vagrant. Foul weather stains of damp stained the walls. People even lived on the landings where crude looking poles for drying washing were rigged out of the windows and a free flow of air was impeded." A fire ladder is parked behind the old Guildhall.

Full length Portraits of George IV by Hopner, George III, Queen Charlotte, and the Prince Consort in the Old Sessions Court before it was converted into the City Library, in 1876. W. H. K. Wright, F.L.A. the city librarian wrote a paper which was delivered to the London conference of Librarians "on the best means of promoting the free library movement in small towns and villages".

PALACE COURT

"As many miserable people as can be crowded in live here. Inside, the occasional old old corbel in the wall and carving concealed by whitewash and the noble oak timbers in the roof show the former importance of the building." It was at this "goodly house towards the haven "that Catherine Princess of Arragon was entertained by a rich merchant, John Paynter, Mayor of Plymouth on her arrival in England, 1501. Rawlinson remarked in 1853 that the external standpipe water was only on for one hour each day. This one served the whole court. "Tubs, pots, pans and troughs were placed in the yard and on the stairs where they absorb all the deleterious gases of the place."

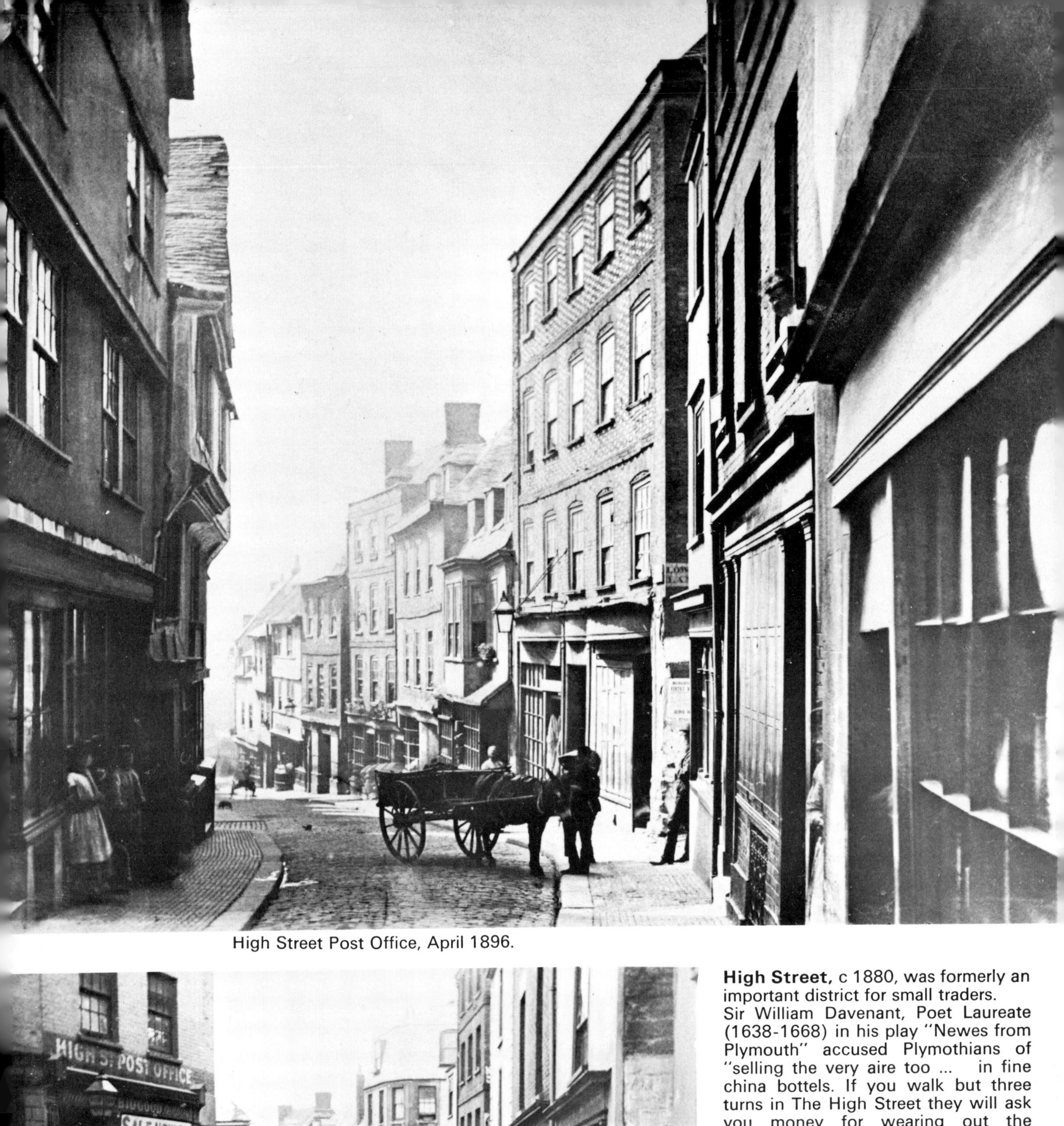

High Street Post Office, April 1896.

High Street, c 1880, was formerly an important district for small traders.
Sir William Davenant, Poet Laureate (1638-1668) in his play "Newes from Plymouth" accused Plymothians of "selling the very aire too ... in fine china bottels. If you walk but three turns in The High Street they will ask you money for wearing out the pebbles."
W. E. J. Parsons (born 1868) who worked as sewerman and foreman from 6 a.m.-5.30 p.m. (Saturdays 4.30) inhaled "the aire" (inflammable sewer-gas) and survived to write about his night shift which started at 8 p.m. From pits eighteen feet apart mud carts were loaded and took their load to Millbridge where "The Dead lake" was being filled in to make Victoria Park. Ladders were put down the manholes to stop the men from being swept away during a storm. For his labours Mr. Parsons received eighteen shillings a week.

High Street, April 1896.
Children played on the pavement with a skipping rope under the birdcage; the hill is too steep for hoops.
A girl with "leg of mutton sleeves" is running down hill towards Gill's Yard where the strawberry carts were kept. Large rats frequented the Quayside, but were ignored by men playing skittles at the back of *The Carpenters Arms* nearby.

The sixteenth century arcade in the passage leading to Nichol's Court, last of the picturesque buildings of High Street, was re-erected behind the flats in 1937. Mr. Jose didn't approve of the practice, not unknown in Plymouth, of leaving an undertaker's card at the home of a sick person.

The varied roof tops of The Parade seen from the new Fish Market where the Town Crier, wearing his tricorne hat (centre), awaits a suitable moment to disclose the contents of the document he holds behind his back. Here, a team of seven or eight men, after shaking the catch out of the nets would hand over "the cargo of silver and gold to the 'herring lassies' who worked late by the light of carbide lamps"

A bugle announced the arrival of the Co-op oil, paraffin and chopped firewood man. A tray with measurements was kept in the back where oil for the larboard range was served from two brass taps. Two bundles of wood cost one penny.
"Donkey Rowe" with his team of six donkeys, (which he lent for Sunday School outings), also sold firewood in the city.
The blacksmith's shop was in Harbour Avenue, not far from the Co-op's warehouse. Nearby, drivers strolled along a platform at high tide whilst taking their horses down into the water for a wash.

QUAY ROAD c 1895

"It is hardly conceivable that anybody coming within one hundred yards of this pest spot could think that he lived in the latter part of the nineteenth century in a town that is supposed to have a sanitary department and a Medical officer of Health. To us who have to work here it is intolerable; many leave the place vomiting."
In 1899 there were also complaints that small children chose to sit round the shaft of the sewer vent; they found entertainment there, when the flap jumped with the force of gas, but they were not deterred by the accompanying stench.

VAUXHALL QUAY AND SUTTON WHARF c 1870

It was possible to walk from North Quay over the boats to the Whitehouse near the Fishmarket when a cargo of timber was landed. In the forground of the picture timber is being seasoned for use as beam trawls. Nearby, barges from Millbrook landed their cargo of bricks; these were chucked onto the quay in pairs.

The Customs House and sail lofts. The railings at The Parade Square and Garrison Green were formerly used for drying sails and nets at herring season. Crocker's sweet shop was lit by an oil lamp and the popular Plymouth humbugs and a sweet called "Old Father Luck" that had a toy inside, were sold here.

THE PARADE 1865

The Creek before the authorities stopped the import of long haired Spanish cattle that were driven ashore at Marrowbone Slip, a less silted part of Sutton Harbour. The photograph of the French brig *Marie Natalie* was taken from the steps at the end of Stokes Lane, where Quay Road was later built. She was moored temporarily mid-harbour after discharging her cargo. A covered waggon stands outside the Customs House, and there is a dockside crane by the stern of the vessel. A Tamar barge is moored near the Three Crowns in a position now occupied by the *Kathleen & May*, the last of the West Country top sail schooners. The bars at the Ship were patronised by Frenchmen too, and the spitoons rang from a fair distance.

NORTH QUAY

"It was three pints for starters" at the *Three Crowns* when piecework was completed. The dockers could carry their beer and frequently pulled out to Rame Head or Penlee to ensure work on incoming ships. Plymouth was one of the principal coaling stations in the English channel, and the big liners coaled here. The planks whipped as men ran to and fro with two hundredweight baskets on their backs. When the coalboat had been discharged, local people dredged the remaining coal.

VAUXHALL QUAY

There was free beer at Sutton Harbour Regatta. This could be a profitable event if the technique of running for a leg of pork or mutton on the end of a greasy pole had been mastered; another event included ducks being dropped off a platform into the water. Boys promptly dived in order to grab their legs. When caught, there was a speedy gullet-slitting session on the quay. The crews of the ice and saltcod boats who were regular visitors to Plymouth were amongst the onlookers.

UNCOALING SHIP, NORTH QUAY 1895

On the quay, women weighed heavy sacks of Guernsey potatoes. Political meetings were held in the open air. The latent strength of the Trade Unions was soon made apparent. On Sundays the religious banners were a regular feature. In the crowd, a man sold carvings of solomon's temple, made specially from Jerusalem timber.

Quay Road, c 1900, thronged with people speaking different dialects; some difficult to understand. The smell of sawdust and beer through the open door of the public bar was a refuge from the noise of clattering winches and baskets of fish rising and falling from the holds.

"Table d'hote daily at 1 p.m. and a hearty welcome to all captains visiting the port . . ." *Luce's Navy Hotel* near the Customs House, Consulate and pier; "master marines, passengers and families will find every accommodation and comfort."
Nearby during election campaigns, Lady Astor tackled the hecklers at close quarters after getting some response when she first addressed a meeting from aboard a fishing smack. At question time one man asked her "how many ribs has a monkey got?"
"Lift up your shirt and count 'em," she retorted.

QUAY ROAD

The smell of Dogfish guts was a cure for asthma. At Whitehouse Pier, men skinned up to a thousand dogfish an hour on hooks with a dextrous movement of the foot and knife; "as easy as taking your coat off."

SOUTHSIDE STREET
Where "rings" were played at the *Queen's Arms*, behind which was Trinity Church that seated 1082, and the school. The editor of *The Western Figaro* whose office was nearby, remarked in August 1882 on the uniform of the soldiers marching down to The Barbican "with the old shakos of the 32nd, surmounted by horse hair plumes, . . . shades of the Duke of Wellington." A more familiar sound was the clogs of the Scottish herring girls as they hurried on their way to their lodgings at Hoegate Street.

MILLMAN'S PAWNSHOP c 1917
G. W. Copeland
At a side door before eight a.m. on a Monday morning, a fisherman's wife, short of money after the weekend would carefully unwrap her husband's best suit and place it in pawn for a few shillings until the following Friday.

THE FISH MARKET c 1900
A woman places a sample of the catch on the floor for inspection. The auctioneer waits with his bell; by his side stands a fish humper. Nearby, Pennycross Bill would entertain people on payment of a penny by turning cart wheels or sticking his head in a butt of water.

QUAY ROAD c 1895
Fish crates belonging to buyers cause congestion after the auction. (Note the bell on the floor). Nearby, the Buzzer, a refuse boat would be moored at the quay waiting to remove the offal before the days of chemical treatment.

SOUTHSIDE STREET c 1898
The inns here were crowded with sea captains discussing stowage. Robert White Stevens listened to them and in 1858 published his solution to their problems; "On stowage of ships and their cargoes". At Mitre Court a vinegar works provided employment for local women; on the corner of Pins Lane opposite *The Albion*, Mr. Warren's bakehouse provided fishermen with their bread at 4 a.m. Sunday dinners were cooked here for 1d. American Centennial Plymouth gin won acclaim, and made the street famous.

"HERRING BOATS UP THE POOL"
The sails are hoisted up the mast after the Saturday catch has arrived. It is also the pilchard season. By the 1890's there was a large fleet of steam trawlers operating from The Barbican, and boats from as far away as Boulogne and Aberdeen brought their catch to Plymouth

THE MORNING FRY OR "STOCKER" 1900
Ernest Phillips, (left,) "Sorter" Forster, and Bill Laurie (right). Their old leather boots were used by the dockers, who split them down and inserted a headpiece. A protective flap for the shoulders was added.

Clay pipes were free in some pubs, or cost a halfpenny. The barber sold cherrywood pipes and charged three farthings.

PINS LANE looking towards Southside Street c 1880 "Ventilation they have none, except at the door". Pins Lane residents were reprimanded in 1853 for "their reckless carelessness in not keeping the drains in order." On their demolition in 1898, only Hewer's Row North Street now survives as an example of traditional fishermen's cottages in Plymouth.

A man wearing a cheesecutter cap unloads shellfish on the Barbican quay.

Fishcarts outside the *North Country Pink* inn awaiting the catch. If trawlers were becalmed, they would miss the Saturday market, the trains to London and the Midlands, and the fish might have to be dumped, or sold for manure. The pubs were open from 6.30 a.m. till 11 p.m., and when a boat came in there were always people watching.

Local herrings were always praised by foreigners, but many also sampled the celebrated congers' liver and mackerell flavoured with bayleaves; "baby's head", (steak pudding with delicious gravy and peas, was also a popular item on the menu.
Barbican women were enterprising: Louisa Sophia Nichols already had managed several pubs when she took over the refreshment house at 12 Barbican in 1914. She also had her own laundry and took in washing from foreign boats.

The Barbican Quay before the fishmarket was built, a photograph contemporary with the painting by W. Gibbons (1893) owned by the Sutton Harbour Improvement Company. Note the dovecote (also depicted by the artist) on the wall of the warehouse in the foreground which was next door to *The Navy Hotel'*.
The Barbican was already known through the paintings of Nicholas Condy and other local artists before it became popular with modern Mayflower pilgrims.

Fishwomen sell the day's catch near the Mayflower steps. Their sense of smell was impaired by regularly taking snuff from linen snuff bags hung round their necks. Fishermen from other towns were also at the quay. On the right is a Brighton boat.

SUTTON HARBOUR BEFORE BREAKFAST

"At five in the morning the cafes are already open and the fishermen have collected freshly baked loaves from the bakery. In the clear morning colour the white and brown of the furled up sails can be appreciated. A few policemen, anxious to be off their beats approach; then postmen hurrying to work. The street sweepers are industriously brooming and a tramp appears from somewhere, glad that the night has gone. In the distance engines lazily puff to and fro as if not particular whether they are going to Exeter or down to Penzance. The Parade Clock point to six and more workmen appear. Presently the sails of the trawlers begin to unfurl and nets are hauled down. The sound of hammer and chisel falls on the still air. In the Barbican work has begun too. Only three or four donkey carts have yet arrived, backed to the edge of the pavement that has to serve as a fish market. Sundry heaps of rays have been flung down; a few bream, pollock and whiting are lying about. A dead turtle is the centre of attraction having been brought in by one of the boats overnight. The poor carcase is kicked, whereas if it had lived to be landed on the Kings Road Brighton, it might have made soup at Muttons and been lauded by the fairest lips. Paddon the fish seller has his first turn this morning. Which means that he has the right to sell his lots a little after seven. Some foreign skippers arrive, bent on an early drink. At *The Dolphin* it is heard that there has been a catch of some twenty-six thousand mackerell the day before. There is a ringing of bells which is a token that the sales are commencing. A crowd of buyers, amongst them one or two ladies with faded blackened eyes, fiery noses and shrill voices scramble over boxes, dodging between the carts to hear the first sale conducted by the youth who first of all bids the buyers "buck up" and then proceeds to sell. An indistinguishable hubbub prevails until some lot is knocked down at £6.6.4d. Another youth strides over the cases and bids the attendants to open them. The ladies do not buy, and whisper words not usually found in the dictionary; they are scarcely audible against the clatter of up to ninety carts drawn by horses, mules or donkeys. Throughout the morning the coffee houses and drink shops have plenty of customers."

As described by *"The Idler", The Western Figaro, May 9th, 1884.*

BARBICAN QUAY c 1864 T. F. K. Rives (negative. No. 45)
A caged bird sings outside the first floor window of Johnson, the ship chandler, at *The Island House*. In 1620, some of the Pilgrim Fathers are said to have lodged here, and the sloping foreshore caused flooding at the ebb tide. The South Gate was only eighteen years old when they walked under the arch to go aboard ship. The rooms above provided a good vantage point to see them depart on Wednesday, 6th September from the point where now the west pier stands. The gatehouse was demolished in 1831, some thirty years before this photograph was taken, on account of the congestion caused by the fish carts, crates and piles of fish. Thomas Jago, landlord of the *Crown* & *Anchor*, his neighbours, Luscombe the butcher and Millman the pawnbroker and outfitter, could remember it standing at the end of the quay. At the watch house lived Constable Fuge, a familiar figure who wore a high silk hat and gleaming brass buttons on his coat. The Barbican was once renowned as a place where policemen ventured only in twos, or even threes and they wouldn't have intervened when an unfortunate man was found stumbling round the quay under the influence of drink by his irate wife, late one night. She promptly unscrewed his wooden leg and administered a sound beating; then indignantly throwing the prostrate body over a fishcart she wheeled him home.
Barbican people worked long hours and their drinking time had not yet been seriously curtailed by the Mission workers preaching temperance.

The Elizabethan House
32 New Street, 1929
Cyril H. Gill

The Island House (left)
c 1917 G. W. Copeland
A street in part as narrow as "The Shambles" in York. Now the frontage have been set back at this point and a view of the quay opened up. Nearby, local women wearing oilskin aprons and small sea boots 'split' for kippers. Most of the smoking was attended to overnight.

George Bryant's ship chandler's shop at The Island House, c 1900
The problem of keeping an historic district in being . . . "Is there any more historic in the kingdom", urged the preservationists when *The Times* featured the clearance scheme that Plymouth corporation envisaged.

WEST PIER c 1840
A detail of an oil painting by James Harris.
"The dark expressive countenances of the Barbican fishermen." Their working clothes were soon to change more radically than the fashions of the worthies standing behind them. Fisherwomen look over the wall beside the Mayflower stone; also included in the picture are Mr. Brooks the Bethel preacher and Constable Fuge (right).

LOOKING DOWN CASTLE STREET TOWARDS THE ORIGINAL MAYFLOWER STEPS AND THE BETHEL, c 1917.
G. W. Copeland
Where the road turns sharp left, there was a patch of grass where traditionally the Pilgrim Fathers stood and prayed prior to embarking. The back of the former *Brunswick Hctel* closes the vista.
In the mornings Barbican women collected washing off ships in the harbour. The young women are standing outside Mrs. Major's mangle shop where elderly people could take their sheets rather than carry them to the public washouse in Hoegate Street. Mrs. Orchard sat on her feather mattress in the small front room of her cottage, always neat, wearing her white waist apron and told fortunes by cards and crystal. The fortunes of the street had changed when this photograph was taken, the roadway no longer muddy and uneven, a place where in 1885 "the wheels of the scavenger's cart had to be locked before the men dare trust the horse to drag it down the street; even so it makes a sidelong crab-like progression." (*Western Figaro*).
The number of beerhouses and pubs diminished as St. Saviour's mission at the crest of the hill made its presence felt in the person of Father Barnes. At *The Jolly Young Waterman* (just out of view on the right) he found "an outrageous scene of immorality", (the details of which he didn't chronicle); Placing his back to the only door that gave access to "Damnation Alley" he said to the soldiers in the room; "are you not ashamed of yourselves, men wearing Her Majesty's uniform to be found in such a disgraceful condition." He caused the inn to be shut up so that the license lapsed. Subsequently there were no more billets for soldiers in beer houses in this district.
It was the beer houses rather than the pubs that welcomed the "squid money" (cuttle fish used as bait) that the trawler apprentices earned. Hence the clause even in a 1916 apprenticeship for sea fishing service that "the Master's goods must not be embezzled or wasted, nor should the apprentice frequent taverns or alehouses, absenting himself from his Master's service without leave."
The fishermen spent much of their leisure time at the Bethel (far right), where they played draughts or dominoes, and smoked their pigtails of tobacco. In the small museum were examples of their best attempts at coaxing ships into bottles, (even into a torchbulb); also framed photographs of ships, the fishing community and bible classes of up to a hundred strong.

Vodden, the Town Crier.

In February 1933, this 125 year old slate-hung building used by customs officials as a watch house for shipping entering Sutton Harbour was demolished. Children who paid brief visits to the Police Station there can recall hearing in this "dark hole of Calcutta" the sound of waves beating against the cells at high tide.

Hookers and a pleasure boat moored in front of the *Brunswick Hotel*, where the rooms over the archway to the left were built over the original Mayflower Steps. Francis Frith's view (c 1890) clearly shows the alterations in the street frontage today.

"Haunted House", adjoining Whitaker's "smokehouse" on Plymouth's Commercial Wharf. The barrel belonging to Joey Jacobs, landlord of *The Navy Hotel* (in Southside Street) who owned the adjoining fishstore that had formerly been part of the eighty-six stores that made up the old Victualling office complex alongside the quays. Through the archway was the washouse where the clothes of the Tucker family, who lived above, were boiled in a large copper on washdays.

Barbican Drinking Fountain; the iron cup gave the water a strangely individual taste. The girl however drinks deep trustingly . . .

A Barbican child's love of water was instilled when at an early age the jet of spray from the water cart, that had been replenished at the Lambhay Hill standpipe, caused their first instant goose-pimples. Other childhood highlights included a skip with friends all the way to the Plympton Ridgeway Bunshop at the crack of dawn on a Good Friday morning.

Whitaker's "smokehouse". Stibbs owned fishing smacks and had a sail loft here. Formerly the Old Victualling Yard here had two bakehouses, with four ovens each that produced ships biscuit that soon became substandard in the unhygenic stores. The old cellars were interconnected by a maze of tunnels and it was impossible for a man to walk upright.

"Mangy seadogs" moored on Phoenix Wharf. The ship in the foreground has special ports for loading and discharging long baulks of timber.

LAMBHAY HILL c 1880
The Missioner and his wife pose with a group of children at the back entrance to the Bethel. The man on the right has the stance of a fisherman. The partly whitewashed house behind them is the only fragment that has survived of the castle commemorated in the Plymouth coat of arms. The women's starched aprons are no longer a familiar sight in the Barbican. In the background is the *Fisherman's Arms*, now standing adjacent to the flats.

"A saloon steamer every twenty minutes from Phoenix Wharf for the Golflinks, Staddon Heights and Bovisand." A voyage beset by the smells of the boneworks at Cattedown, Serpell's biscuit factory baking, and the stench of fish offal.

"They possessed a true Amazonian spirit and a courage foreign to their sex . . ." Women managed the boats that brought farmers and villagers to market at Plymouth before the red funnelled Plymouth & Oreston boats cornered their business in 1871. Here the *Lively* departs from Phoenix Wharf.

THE HOE AND CITADEL c 1870
When the Citadel was no longer used as a fortress there were plans to demolish it and extend the Hoe Park. This view clearly shows the undeveloped foreshore, the Trinity Obelisk later replaced by Smeaton's Tower, and the lower fort before the Royal Plymouth Corinthian Yacht Club was built.
The lamplighter on his morning round, unlocking the gate to the adjoining "Cage Walk" would on Wednesday morning see barges laden with luggage leaving the Colonial Government depot's wharf where the mess room walls were decorated with posters depicting colonial life. Those beginning their assisted passages were handed a copy of *The Emigrant's Penny Magazine*, Plymouth's "helping hand of Christian sympathy". At Fisher's Nose nearby, the tradition of presenting "the Freedom Boys" with a "piece of money" was enacted every year by the Mayor, sword bearer and serjeants at mace.

Rugg Monk
Only sailing trawlers moored midharbour, making use of the chains on the side of the East and West Piers to get under way.

LAIRA BRIDGE
Fishing was not discouraged at Laira Bridge whereas it was frowned upon at the halfpenny gate at Stonehouse. James Meadows Rendel was a "young and almost untried man" when he designed the five hundred foot, five arched bridge, completed in 1827. The cast iron was the work of a Shropshire ironmaster, but the stonework was by local contractors.
The *Englishman* is moored in the foreground.

Serpell's Biscuit Factory, Lambhay Wharf was sold by auction in 1899 and their horse drawn waggons were no longer seen in Plymouth. In 1934 a new road linked The Hoe and The Barbican and these buildings were demolished.

A view of the Watch House (far right) and a hand winch on the wharfside. Horse-drawn ambulances came here bringing patients to the fever ship, the *Maud*. The other hospital ship morred in Jennicliffe Bay was the *Pique*, later replaced by H.M.S. *Flamingo*, which was subsequently part of The Defiance Group.

"Tamar Steamer".

NORTH ROAD STATION TO THE HALFPENNY BRIDGE, STONEHOUSE

North Road Station, 1877.
The first station master received £2 for a seven day week. There was a lot of rail traffic going over the wooden viaduct at Pennycomequick, but the tunes played by the organ grinder under the arch could be heard above the rumble. The assistant who held out the cap as visitors to the circus at Exhibition Fields nearby passed her by recalled the "occasionally a well dressed girl would come towards me gracefully and having tossed her beautiful tresses over her shoulder, placed a coin in the cap with an air of a princess".

The Roman Catholic Cathedral, North Stonehouse, and the remaining meadows between Cecil Street and Wyndham Square, 1858.
The spire that Baring Gould described as "a lanky stalk of asparagus" was added later. Artizans lived in this district. Signors Fazi at Eldad Place and John Pellegrini of Stoke Hill were plaster figure makers.

The Tollkeeper's Cottage, Millbridge in the days when the owners of horse and carts had to pay 2d. for a ticket, valid that day only, to come to and from Devonport.

As it got dusk, the billposter man was seen at work supplying posters in two layers. It was expected that the opposition from other cinemas would follow him round peeling off his handywork before it had had a chance to dry.

The double gibbet stood near here, but was taken down in 1827. At this time the Parish sexton and a Millbridge tradesman sold fresh corpses from the graveyard to local hospitals who asked no questions about where they had obtained them. The bodysnatchers were subsequently informed upon, and the sexton took his life. A wooden doll known to have been placed in the arms of a little girl at burial was found in the tradesman's possession and he was transported for life.
Stoke church had the reputation among sailors of being the West Country equivalent of Gretna Green. Their brides were led up the long processional porch (see right) to inevitable unhappiness. The Royal Military Hospital (left) where "the internal arrangements are based on the most liberal principles" had its own landing stage.

Military Hospital, 1855.

"I break rope yarn, spun yarn and copper wire with the muscle of my bare arm." The entertainment also included balancing a cart wheel and throwing it into the air, putting the weight with a spatula between his teeth and the son threw a miniature spear into Victoria Park.

Side Show, Plymouth Races, 1900.

Fox & Elliott's Timber pond (far right), "Tinkies", where children who played there in their Sunday clothes had to learn to be surefooted, Millbridge tidemill and beyond, the "evil smelling mudflats of the 'Dead Lake'." A high wall still screens the Naval hospital burial yard at No Place, and St. Dunstan's Abbey which was built for the Anglo Catholics is a masterpiece in Plymouth limestone by the Victorian master architect of texture William Butterfield.

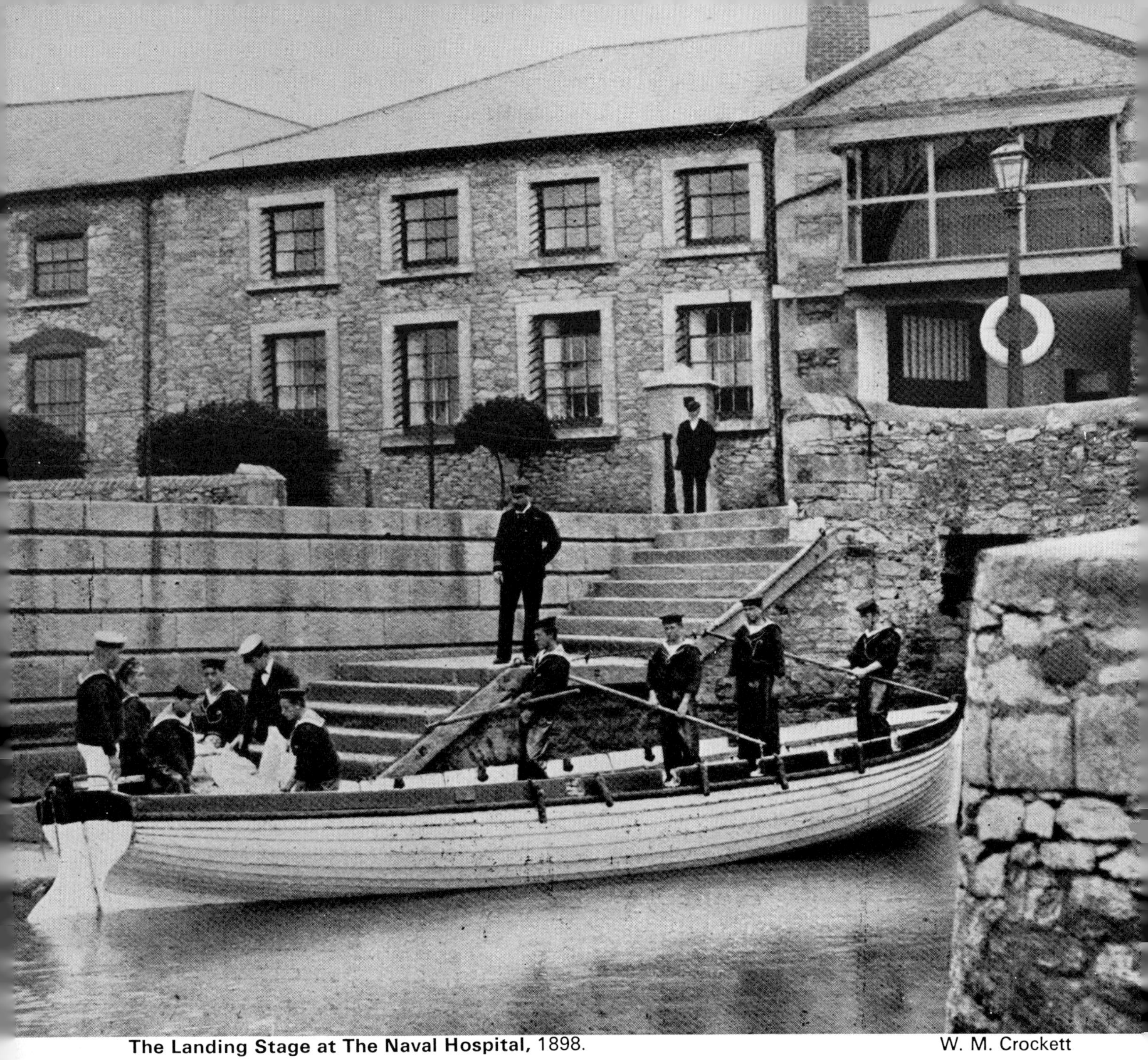

The Landing Stage at The Naval Hospital, 1898. W. M. Crockett

The difficulties involved in landing a cot case "cannot well be got over until some inventive genius perfects a process of aerial locomotion."
Water transport was the quickest means of conveying patients here, and The Nightingale and Cavell, hospital boats, were a familiar sight in The Hamoaze.

Old Houses at Smeaton's Halfpenny Bridge, Stonehouse. In 1799, a Royal Marine who had committed suicide was buried at the crossroads with a stake through his heart.
There were over thirty watermen's boats moored here, and the river played an important part in most people's lives. This was the departure point for Cawsand; children dived into the murky water and retrieved halfpennies wrapped up in silver paper. Nearby stood Dusty Brown the Sword Swallower; the sound of Hancock's whirligig in Richmond Walk struck a festive note for the passer-by.

Millbridge tidemill, 1899. J. Boolds
While Victoria Park was being created, clay dams were put under the bridge by sewermen to prevent the tide coming in.
Local people were nervous when passing here at night. A man had hung himself in the echoing shell of the building. At Millbridge boat station each passenger was allowed ½ cwt. Swiss's Official Naval & Military Directory of the Three Towns monthly quoted the fares of the watermen and cabmen. A charge was made for additional baggage, and "foul weather fares" were by agreement.

Halfpenny Gate, Stonehouse, and Lidstone's hording
Boys waited for non servicemen to pass through and begged their return ticket, or alternatively ran through on the blind side of the tram.
In the ticket office little Maudy Burchell sat on a high stool and took the toll money.

"The warrens of the poor". The back of old houses in High Street, Stonehouse, c 1930.
"Nearly everyone accustomed to walk from Devonport to Plymouth is acquainted with the many scenes of debauchery that stare them in the face after passing the Stonehouse bridge gate. Publicans were threatened by the withdrawal of their licences for harbouring prostitutes, and the ladies were all told this Saturday to look for shelter at the workhouse, and they went there four deep beating tin kettles and blowing tin whistles. "Mr. Cox explained "that he couldn't take all of them although he added that he had plenty of oakum for them to pick." On Monday they found new quarters in Devonport."

"The sleepy hollow of the old Plymouth life." Captain Scott.
Old age pensioners at Devonport Park, c 1900. In the afternoons they sat here and sang songs.

Bicycle Races, Raglan Barracks, 1884.
The days when gentlemen cyclists wore swallow-tail coats and high silk hats.

Peel Street, a meeting place for tradesmen of all kinds. There were few houses that didn't have Royal Marine families. The officer of the day toured the streets with the marriage roll and asked if there were any complaints. A bugler sounded the mobilisation call from street corners.

Emma Place, a fashionable street where carriages could regularly be seen outside the houses of solicitors and other professional gentlemen. Stone Hall (right) 1769, was demolished in 1963.

The residence at No. 1 Durnford Street of Dr. George Budd M13 who helped to formulate Conan Doyle's methods of deduction. Whilst he was staying there it is possible that he might have read the old story about "the monstrous Newfoundland dog that had been shot on April 19th, 1843 after creating havoc amongst the flocks, sucking their blood at Tavy Cleave . . ."

Fish hawker, St. Mary's Street. The Naval Hospital gates still remain, although the old houses have now been replaced by flats. Nearby was the weigh house belonging to the forage merchants John Hitchins who supplied Granby Barracks and The Royal Marine barracks.

The Link boy and the tram on Devonport Hill. On the skyline is the palladian St. George's Hall. Later the Devonport & Stonehouse Electric works supplied electricity for the trams, from 1901.

The Brickfields, Devonport. Francis Frith

"The bright sunlight made the swords and bayonets flash; the steel barrels of the Naval field guns shone like silver." Godfrey Wycisk.

The last pageant was held here on June 3rd, 1913. The Brickfields were flat until The Kaiser's War.

May 19th, 1871. The Duke of Edinburgh returned from a cruise on Galatea. His mascot, Tommy an elephant led the procession up Fore Street to The Devonport Mechanic's Institute and his elderly friend Anne Glanville the Saltash oarswoman were guests at a dinner for the crew.

C. B. Courtenay Thomas.

Accountant and Auditor, Devonport.

Who well looked after the Ratepayers interest in showing up overcharges and illegal payments when auditing the Devonport Corporation accounts, and endured any amount of persecution for so doing.

C. B. C. Thomas, Devonport. No. 2.

The Royal William Victualling Yard, c 1868.
Duprez
Water boats filled up from the Navy reservoir at Devil's Point en route for India. It was only recently that the Navy discontinued training coopers. At the trussol ceremony, five year apprentices were coated with soot and sawdust and rolled round the yard in a warm barrel.
On the left are the Royal Clarence Baths where bathing machines could be hired out. The old slate-hung cottages have since been demolished.

The Admiral's Yacht, H.M.S. *Vivid*, c 1898.
Rugg Monk
The Admiral's Steps can still be seen at Mount Wise. Out of view (right) was the old signalling station. The one o'clock time signal operated nearby.
On the left can be seen the roofs of Mutton Cove, Bullock's Dock and Candle bay (so named after the amount of ship's candle that could be found washed up in the vicinity. Sausage skins were made here and the stench wafted up to the promenaders.

Ocean Quay and Admiral's Hard, c 1898.
Rugg Monk
The Sulphur works have recently been demolished. In 1905, the S.W.R. were running The Ocean "special" that got to Waterloo in just over four hours. It took only twenty-one minutes from Cawsand bay to get through the Customs on to the train here.

Old Houses, Mutton Cove. c 1898.

The Landing Place, Mutton Cove, c 1868. Duprez
"The landing place was crowded with boats, and it was not without sundry exchanges of foul words and oaths, the bow-man dashing the point of his boathook into the shore boats that we forced our way on to the beach. The bowman said that his wife was on the wharf with his clothes from the wash begged leave to go and fetch them. I refused, saying that she could bring them to him. 'Vy, now, Mr. Simple', said the woman, 'arn't you a nice lady's man, to go for to ax me to muddle my way through all the dead dogs cabbage stalks and stinking hakes' heads with my bran new shoes and clean stockings'. It was very dirty and wet and I didn't like to refuse her, and the shingle was strewed with all that she had mentioned." Captain Marryat. *Peter Simple.*

Mutton Cove looking towards Clarence Stairs (far right) the site of the old Cremyll ferry. Royalty landed there. The provision boats sometimes encountered rough seas, and if the men took too many "parting glasses" the cargo might get damaged if they overloaded the boats.

The Capella from Fowey moored at Mutton Cove, c 1868. Duprez

Devonport boys serving their apprenticeship at Waterman's yard (now Mashfords) left Mutton Cove every morning at 7 a.m. in a forty foot ex-service cutter. The first job was to drag trees into the saw mill for sawing on the rollers of the frame saw.
The photograph of the staff of the yard clearly shows the half model, of one of the ships they are building.

Watermen's boats and the once sloping Cremyll beach. Orphanage children were landed here by the Navy launch and taken up to "The Big House" by waggonettes where the Earl and Countess of Mount Edgcumbe provided donkey rides and a strawberry and cream tea.

The Hamoaze, c 1880.
At the entrance to The Hamoaze was The Vanguard Rock which H.M.S. *Cambridge* removed with a fourteen foot cylinder containing a ton of gun powder which was held in store for use in The Crimea. "The Dammed Reserve" (surplus vessels) were painted yellow and roofed in to preserve the timbers. Much shipbuilding was carried out under government supervision at private yards in Plymouth before 1890. Schooners were built from old timbers of men of war at Victoria Wharves, Cattedown. The Naval fleet moored here until after World War II. During fleet manoeuvres at night, attempts were made to steer close to the shore without being seen; although many searchlights were scanning The Sound.

Mutton Cove and houses in James Street, c 1900.
Rugg Monk
The Boy Sam (the third boat back) may still be seen in the cove. Eighteen foot boats built before 1940 took part in the Gala and Carnival.

Abrahams

29th October, 1914. The last meeting of The Devonport Council. Clifford Tozer was the youngest councillor. To the right stood Foulston's Moorish Mount Zion Chapel with its bulbous minarets; it became The Salvation Army temple with seats for 1,400. From here they sallied forth to persuade sailors to put a penny on the drum on Saturday nights.

Devonport Fire Brigade, 1904.

Geo. Bayley

Shoe Black Boy, Gamlen Brothers' Corner, Fore Street. Francis Frith

"The shop made a very cosy restaurant with settles. I had bright colours mirrors and a little gilding, for I was competing against public houses," wrote Agnes Weston in 1874. Until the blitz Fore Street pubs offered a good game of darts and skittles. Bluejackets staying at *The Sailor's Rest* if the worse for wear were put into "Aggie's Strongbox" to sober up. Near the Dockyard gate the "Banana Queen" and "Monkey Brand" sold fruit. Rock-o-Bob gave lollipops and windmills, in exchange for rags. Devonport was a self sufficient shopping centre. The Market in Tavistock Street could provide the best from the Tamar Market gardens and had a special cut flower section. Nearby were slogans advising no spitting; the pub's spittoons however rang from a fair distance.

Morshead's Royal Hotel, Fore Street. Francis Frith

Looking from the cab rank towards The Devonport Public Hall later The Electric Theatre. At The Hippodrome Guy Prance had local talent featuring in matinee shows. Emminent people were happy to be filmed expressing love, horror and hate as this master of farce directed.

The Corner Shop, James Street and Ordnance Row.
J. Blake

Old fashioned sweets were on sale here: "Kruger's whiskers", little shreds of coconut sweetened and coloured brown with chocolate were displayed between "Spanish shoe-laces", bags of sherbert, everlasting sticks of toffee and liquorish. Gobstoppers were black and patterned like an eye when sucked.

Street games included "kick stone trot", "flyboy", "relieve oh", "Jack o Lantern", Jump Back", "spinning tops", "five stones", "cherry odds" and a home made rag ball.

At 10.45 on a Sunday morning the girls marched in pairs to St. Michael's Church. Nearby was Exmouth House School where Captain Scott attended as a day pupil.

Female orphanage for the daughters of soldiers and sailors, Navy Row (Albert Road), c 1868. Duprez

"Before breakfast at 8 a.m. young children cleaned cutlery with brickdust on a board while older children cleaned the flues, scrubbed the huge kitchen range and then blackleaded it, holystoned the hearth which came up pure white and the steel fender shone like silver after monkey brand. Meals were eaten in silence; breakfast consisted of porridge on three mornings, bread and dripping on other days. The girls were trained for service and made their own clothes including their black knitted stockings. All garments and linen were starched and ironed, goffered and polished with a round edged iron to get a shiney effect. When they left the orphanage their service uniform consisted of two alpaca dresses for the afternoon, two floral prints for work, two afternoon aprons, two morning aprons mob caps and cuffs and the prospect of wages amounting to 7/6d. per month."

Physical exercises in the playground with Alf Day, an ex army physical training instructor. "We enjoyed it because he kept us at it."
In summer the girls wore flannel petticoats and white aprons.

"**Liberty men ashore**". North Corner, c 1900. Rugg Monk
In 1925 a sixteen years old waterman rowed twenty men ashore after they had paid off. They passed the cap around and 2/4d. was his reward. The number of watermen decreased before 1939; many suffered from heart trouble. "Peggy" Rickard always wore a skipper's hat when he rowed the Devonport photographer James Abrahams out to the ships.

"Moscow", the self styled "fiery king", spent his most comfortable nights aboard "*The Invera*", hired from the Norris family of Moon Cove by Captain Scott.

The Torpoint Ferry (1878-1926) could take five or six coaches with their teams of horses at a time. The Falmouth to Devonport Mail was always on the last ferry at 9.30 p.m. having rushed the last few miles. One night the offleader fell down dead on arrival: "there the poor fellow lay on his back with his trotters in the air. We made a temporary harness to drive tandem fashion and on arriving at the Devonport side I gave a regular good long loud whistle just to comfort the drooping spirits of his companions. I was driving off, when, it's as true as this whip's a whip, the dead hoss let down his legs and shook himself. By George I was frightened a bit, but I got down, looked at 'n, rubbed'n down and saw that he was all alive, then clapped'n in the harness and drove away. He wasn't nowise the worse for dying. I fancy that it was a super human thing just to show what mare hosses was capable of before the railway came down and knocked them up altogether." The Coachman's Story (Royal Pantomorph, Vol. 1, no. 1, Nov. 28th, 1866.)

The Earl of Mount Edgcumbe lays the memorial stone at The Royal Albert Hospital, June 17th, 1862.
After the Contagious Diseases Act was passed, the hospital had to admit patients who had venereal disease; they were treated more like criminals and locked in their rooms. The hospital benefitted by voluntary donations, and on "Hospital Saturday" a procession of decorated vehicles were accompanied by clowns on stilts who collected money.
The variety of ships in The Hamoaze hadn't changed since Captain Marryat wrote in "The Three Cutters"; "You will see ships building and ships in ordinary; ships repairing and fitting, hulks and convict ships, the guardship . . . lighters, men-of-war's boats, Dockyard boats and shoreboats." Mrs. Williams the principal bum boat officer from Mutton Cove sold loaves, cheese and shaving gear, and tailors took orders off the ships.

A five masted ironclad and Keyham Steamyard (left).
Ships laid off Moon Cove and Pottery Quay took street sweepings and sewage up river.

Rugg Monk

North Corner, c 1898, where a ferry plied to Millbrook. Since 1963, the Dockyard Flyover has obscured this view.

NORTH CORNER

Tamar valley plums and cherries, packed by the grower arrived here for the Devonport Market by steamer early in the morning. Dray horses found the ascent of the Cornwall Street slope (left) difficult. Here lived Robert Hunt who kept a chemist shop at number twelve 1837-40. A Devonport man, he wrote the first book in England on photography: "A popular treatise on the art of photography including Daguerreotype & all the new methods of producing pictures by the chemical agency of light", 1841.

"Swabey-I-Oh"
A Morice Town celebrity who lived on his wits. In appearance and manner he resembled Buster Keaton.

MORICE TOWN

The "Three Towns" were renown for their rivalry. Morice Town children virtually patrolled their boundary, and some didn't travel far. Miss Elizabeth Norris minded boats for her family at Moon's Cove. She left school at twelve and "came straight home to the scrubbing brush". The hire of the bathroom with two washbasins and towels cost sixpence per hour. In front of Joll's Cottages were ladders to the boats. An outrigger cost four shillings per day to hire. At the entrance to the cove the watermen were occasionally called back by the parrot whose whistle was mistaken for an extra passenger requiring their services. On Friday afternoon the children could practise the "corkscrew" dance to the music of the barrel organ. At Harvey's coal wharf at the Tamar Canal men and women worked on into the night by the light of naptha flares staggering across the three planks to and fro with the mawns of coal until their work was done. "The forty pubs" of Morice town were a testimony to their thirst.

At the Morice Town Fair there was "wrestling cudgelling and jingling." The proprietors Sophia and William Hancock were locally based at Richmond Walk. Sophia wore bizarre clothes with colours that clashed, and a hat with the occasional ostrich feather. William was called "pegleg" after an injury in 1895 and rode in a dogcart, the door of which was fastened back so that he could let his wooden leg protrude. White ponies that appeared in his show were kept at Sibley's stables Mutton Cove. Other attractions included a midget race and reflecting mirrors showing only the head. Nearby, Dusty Brown the sword swallower challenged children to hear the marbles rattle in his stomach.

J. Ward, Boatswain, R.N. (retired) of Morice Town who wrote the life saving rules that were taught by all R.N. training ships.

Wightman
The Albert Road Gate to H.M. Dockyard. The horse trolley carried the mid day feed of bran, chaff and oats. John Hitchins' horse teams pulled Dockyard waggons until 1958.

The community spirit.
Granby Street, Plymouth Week, July 1927.

Albert Road Gates where at every outmuster from the yard, hungry children begged "any old lefts Sir?" of a pasty or sandwich. "Chippy" Norman sold large penny scoops of delicious salted chips. Boys occasionally crept up and thrust turfs down the flue on the roof of the waggon. The Yard was on average twelve feet below street level. Now only one of the gatetowers remain. The trees and the forecourt where crowds gathered to hear the Salvation Army band have gone.

"The channel tunnel". On the right is one of Hancock's circus caravans. Sophia Hancock's caravan was painted red and crowded with ornaments and cut glass. At Richmond Walk, the Hancock's hired out gondolas which were suited to the relatively placid waters of The Sound

Swingboats at Hancock's Fair. Note the young woman's shawl and the children's pinafore.

The legs of Brunel's wooden viaduct firmly radiate out into the mud on cast iron shoes. Each crossbound section could be unbolted and renewed.

Camel's Head Creek, c 1895 Rugg Monk
A surprising variety of wild birds once visited these tidal waters.

The undeveloped sky-line of Lower St. Budeaux.
The Saltash Ferry and an "Inside" gaff rigged Tamar barge. These vessels were used to transport copper, timber, bricks and lime. The "*Myrtle*" owned by Harold Longsford a miller plied between Cotehele Quay and Plymouth.

Rugg Monk
"What is going on behind teacher's back?", c 1898.
Miss Cross and her pupils from Bull Point school on the beach at Saltash Passage. Local people once harvested the nourishing seaweed.

The Horse boat at Saltash was kept as a standby when the boilers of the steam ferry were being overhauled. The horses were stabled in Wolseley Road.

Fred Cole and Sam, a prize winning carthorse, at St. Budeaux Square.

A sweep with five foot brushes in the countryside outside Plymouth.

Ann Glanville of Saltash, c 1875.
Her lady rowers were invited to foreign regattas. Their health was enthusiastically drunk in champagne by French municipal authorities. She carried eighty bags of corn in her boat from Sutton Pool up the river beyond The Royal Albert Bridge, single handed.

The Royal Albert Bridge, c 1865.
The first train crossed the bridge on 11th April, 1859. It was an object of awe and wonder. Many old people were too frightened to make the journey. Wood & Tozer of Devonport printed a souvenir of its construction and the penny history was on sale at railway bookstalls.

"Although you speak of your 'Three Towns" we know one straggling community." Brunel was aware of local rivalries and not surprised when his proposal for the most central site for a railway terminus at No Place near Millbridge was rejected because Plymouth shopkeepers were afraid of loosing trade to Devonport. He had already worked as engineer to the Millbay Docks where despite difficulties in gradient he later brought the railway. His plans for a floating dock at Sutton Pool, with lockgates on the site of the West Pier, and a train ferry at Torpoint were not carried out to the detriment of the city. William Kingdom, his grandfather, a Naval contractor, was a Freeman of the Borough, and Brunel liked South Devon. It gave him pleasure to design a rustic bridge for his estate at Watcombe, Torquay.

Isambard Kingdom Brunel 1857. A reportage photograph by Robert Howlett.

Coalboat at Ware's Wharf St. Budeaux, c 1910
It was cheaper to have the coal come by sea from the Durham coalfields. Marshall Ware photographed here with his sister remembers the large number of boats then using the Tamar. His father's wharf was later purchased by The Admiralty.

At the inter training ship challenge cup race above Saltash bridge "there was more excitement than at the Oxford and Cambridge boat race", with the crews of The *Defiance, Lion* and other training establishments taking part. Captain Harkcom of *The Mount Edgcumbe* training ship was an enthusiastic oarsman and gave the boys much encouragement On the Devon bank is Newland House used as the ship's hospital.

The cries of boys strapped to a grid for birching were heard by Saltash residents. Until a letter was put in *The Saltash Gazette* explaining that the boys were not bad, many inhabitants would cross the road from them.

The Boys' Band of The Training Ship *Mount Edgcumbe*.

THE ROYAL NAVY AT DEVONPORT

The launching of the battlecruiser H.M.S. *Lion,* 1912, with a complement of 1000 officers and men who later fought at the Battle of Jutland. She could travel at 28 knots.

The girls from The United Services Orphanage were present at a launching. A few were given a piece of rope from the ship. This launching ceremony was filmed, and there was a beautiful sunset afterwards. The boatyards picked up the tallow afterwards.

Officers of H.M.S. *Indus*. Captain Rawson and the "power house" of the Commander and first Lieutenant. There are four Royal Marines and the Chaplain. H.M.S. *Indus* was formerly moored at the north end of Keyham Yard, alongside H.M.S. *Vengeance*.

Rugg Monk c 1901.
A "flying kite" hove to west of The Breakwater with young sub-lieutenants instructing. The decline of the sailing Navy limited the active services of the brigs which were the last naval vessels to work under sail. The students were all from the training ships in The Hamoaze and whilst away were on a diet of bacon, suet pudding and treacle.

Boys from H.M.S. *Impregnable* working aloft. In the early morning the bedding airing in the rigging was a familiar sight. On The *Colussus* (part of The Impregnable group) the routine before breakfast was grim: 0530 Hands were called. Tubs of water were in the open casements for washing in; the ice had to be broken before use. "Lash up and stow hammocks", cocoa and biscuits. Hammocks were inspected before stowing. 0600 Hands, fall in—scrub decks on hands and knees. 0700 breakfast included 3 oz. of good corned pork.
In the early days of the silent films Frank Mundell showed a film by candlelight on board, in the presence of the Admiral. The outward journey was in the Admiral's yacht. Permission to go ashore was granted, but the projectionist had to make his own way . . . and wait in the rain for a boat.

Recruiting station in full swing, 1901. William Crockett
The three men on the right are the first recruits in Great Britain for the new electrical rating. The requirement "robustness of frame" accounted for the failure rate of 40%.

H.M.S. ***Queen*** **at Keyham Steamyard**
October 1853.
H.M.S. *Implacable* (ex Duguay Trouin) had served at Trafalgar before it later became the first training ship in the Royal Navy and was stationed at Devonport in 1860. H.M.S. *Lion* was connected by a gangway in 1871 and her mast and spars were left for use to drill aloft. The waterpolice were on the alert to warn civilian boats when the six and nine o'clock guns were fired from H.M.S. *Lion*.
To the right can be seen H.M.S. *Foudroyant* of 1798 which was a tender to H.M.S. *Cambridge*. Later, destroyers were moored between Torpoint and Wilcove at "The Trot". Other waterborne establishments were H.M.S. *Defiance*, (the torpedo, electrical and mining school and H.M.S. *Cambridge*. The Royal Naval Engineering College at Keyham was formerly based in that wooden hulk H.M.S. *Marlborough* at Portsmouth.

H.M. Training ships H.M.S. *Lion* and *Implacable* moored in The Hamoaze.

Merryweather's Sutherland fire engine was in use until 1905. After the disastrous fire that destroyed the wooden Adelaide gallery the Admiralty purchased this fire engine when it went on show at The Crystal Palace because it was considered to be the most powerful in the world at the time.
Metropolitan Police (see left and right) also manned the Dockyard gates until the Admiralty Police were installed. St. Loe's church with its fine peal of bells (1817) was destroyed in The Blitz.

Devonport Dockyard, c 1855.
The problem of a surfeit of sailing ships.
In 1846 the Dockyard College was set up in South Yard to give tuition regarding steam technology and gave it preference over sail. By 1859 there were guns available that before whose irresistable bolts oak had become feeble and defenceless Wooden ships were regarded as a little better than heaps of firewood. With the advent of iron shipbuilding, roofs were no longer required over building slips. Till that time wooden ships had been allowed to remain for years in the frame so that the sappy timber could be removed before the planking was put on.

The Dockyard Train, c 1901
The carriages were made by Dockyard craftsmen.

The Dockyard Traction Engine, c 1890. R. W. Skilton
"Old Jumbo" rolled into the dock at South Yard.
Nearby in the Engineers' Department "there are engines of great power. The variety of the work they accomplish puzzles the uninitiated who may well fancy themselves transported in a dream to the forges of the Cyclops and exposed to the blast of the underworld."

Chief Porter, R.N.E.C. Keyham, 1891.
J. S. Constable
"On no account should moustaches be allowed without beards. This must be clearly understood." V.R.

"For months at a stretch their engineering vision is bounded by studs, bolts, locks and valves." It was felt that in 1893 that most store articles were being obtained from the students. All the machines were working. Notice the shaft overhead and the belts for different speeds.

THE ROYAL NAVAL ENGINEERING COLLEGE KEYHAM, DEVONPORT

Sword practice, 1891. R. W. Skelton

The fifth year students rowed across The Hamoaze every morning and at the Naval Gunnery grounds did squad drill, rifle or pistol practice and cutlass exercise. The Engineer students took part in the local regattas and had a sailing cutter, the Polly. One of the dry docks was flooded for the swimming sports. There was one competition for fully clothed swimmers to divest themselves of all their clothes in the water and place them all on the floating pontoon. The athletic sports was a social occasion, and the fancy dress chosen for the donkey race "caused any amount of merriment".

(Note the knee pads for different positions in rifle drill.)

Select Bibliography

Decorative detail from proscenium arch, Palace Theatre.

"Story's the light of time for after ages, and books are lanthorns which their light encages."

Bracken, C. W.
A History of Plymouth and her neighbours. Plymouth, Underhill, 1931.
Broderick Index of Devonport (Mss).
Collier, W.
Some sixty years' reminiscences of Plymouth. (In Reports of The Devonshire Association, 1892, Vol. 24, p 86-95)
English, E. (Ed.)
Plymouth of living memory. Plymouth Guild of Social Services, booklet No. 1, 1971.
Gaskell-Brown, C. (Ed.)
A guide to the Industrial archaeology of Plymouth and Millbrook, Cornwall. Plymouth, W.E.A., 1973.
Gill, C.
Sutton Harbour. Plymouth, Sutton Harbour Improvement Company, 1970.
Gill, C.
Plymouth 1848-1958. Plymouth, Y.M.C.A., 1958.
Harris, J.
An essay towards the history of Plymouth . . . written for the use and amusement of my children. 2 Vols. Mss, 1815.
Hine, J.
The old buildings of Plymouth. (In Trans. of Plymouth Institution 1860, Vol. 1, p 13-48.)
(IBID 1877, Vol. 6, p 413-417).
Hunt, W.
Then and now: or fifty years of newspaper work. London, Hamilton Adams, 1887.
Jewitt, L.
A history of Plymouth. Plymouth, Luke, 1873.
Lattimore, M. I.
A study of Plymouth: a survey of its physical historical and economic geography. University of Exeter M.A. Thesis, 1958.
Lewis, M.
A Cornish waif's story. London, Odhams Popular Bookclub, 1954.
Plymouth Comet. Plymouth, Keys, 1893.
Stephens, W.
The highways and byeways of Plymouth; the reminiscences of Walter Stephens. Plymouth, A. C. Brown, 1943.
Trewin, J.
Portrait of Plymouth. London, Hale, 1973.
Wallis, F.
Gone are the days: the reminiscences of Fernley Wallis. Plymouth, 1963.
Weekes, S.
My personal recollections of Plymouth in the late 'fourties. Plymouth, Brendon, 1925.
Welch, C. E.
A guide to the Archives Department of Plymouth City Libraries, 1962.
Western Figaro
1882-1900.
Whitfeld, H. F.
Plymouth and Devonport in times of war and peace. Devonport, Hiorns & Miller, 1900.
Wightwick, George
Guide to Plymouth, Stonehouse and Devonport. Plymouth, Nettleton, 1836.
Worth, R. N.
The Three Towns Bibliotheca: a catalogue of books, pamphlets papers written by natives . . . Plymouth, 1872.
Worth, R. N.
Calendar of Plymouth municipal records. Plymouth, 1893.
Worth, R. N.
History of Plymouth from the earliest period to the present day. Plymouth, Brendon, 1890.

"There is something grimly interesting in these long ranges of heavy ordnance and in the vast pyramids of cannon balls piled up between them". (1874) Men cleaning shot outside store 16, The Gunwharf, c 1855.